F
Lev

Levine, Peter.

The rabbi of swat.

50545

DATE			

The Rabbi of Swat

Peter Levine

Michigan State University Press

East Lansing

The paper used in this publication meets the minimum
requirements of ANSI/NISO Z39.48–1992 (R 1997) ∞

Michigan State University Press
East Lansing, Michigan 48823-5202

04 03 02 01 00 99   1 2 3 4 5 6 7 8 9

LIBRARY OF CONGRESS CATALOGING-IN-PUBLICATION DATA
Levine, Peter.
    The rabbi of swat / Peter Levine.
    p.   cm.
    ISBN 0-87013-517-1 (alk. paper)
    I. Title.
    PS3562.E8997 R33 1999
    813'.54—dc21
                                                99-6026
                                                CIP

This book is a work of fiction. Names, characters, places, and
incidents are either products of the author's imagination or
are used fictitiously.

John Kieran's poem about Babe Ruth's sixtieth home run,
copyright © 1927 by The New York Times Co. reprinted by
permission.

Book design by Sharp Des!gns, Inc.
Cover design by Ariana Grabec-Dingman.

Visit Michigan State University Press on the World Wide Web at:
www.msu.edu/unit/msupress

In celebration of
Ruthie and Matt

Acknowledgments

Different friends read this book for me in different ways. For a long time, I imagined that they would be the only ones who would read it. I valued their advice and their encouragement. Without them, I never would have completed it. Mike Steinberg, Bob Lipsyte, Richard White, Harry Reed, Barry Gross, Eric Fretz and Tilden Edelstein read early drafts and offered critical advice about character and plot. Philip Spitzer, my agent, offered early encouragement and support throughout.

My cousin Jeffrey Goldberg and Arthur Greenspan, my friend since third grade, also offered careful and useful criticism. As always, my wife Gale, listened with a keen ear to a good deal of this book as I wrote it. Although the world I have created is fictional, they, more than anyone, know the real experiences that fueled my imagination.

My daughter, Ruth, who grew up in East Lansing and now lives in Brooklyn, and my cousin, Sonny Levine, who grew up on Sackman Street and now lives in New Jersey, helped me clarify fiction against fact.

Prologue

EMPLOY YOUR imagination. I know I've been dead since 1948. But shit, do you think I would forget my 100th birthday? Me, the guy historians dubbed the hero of excess and who sportswriters called the Sultan of Swat? Not a chance.

You see, I've read everything that's ever been written about me, not just the sports pages when I was playing, but Creamer, Sobol, Smelser, Crepeau and the like—seen all the movies with everyone from William Bendix to John Goodman playing my ass and even ones like *Field of Dreams* that had the chutzpah to leave me out of the cornfields and that conveniently forgot to put me on that cockamamy baseball field in the middle of nowhere.

Surprised? Sure, you would be, if you believed only what you've read and seen. Yes, it's true, I was a narcissistic son of a bitch who ate too much, screwed a lot of women, and loved good times. And yes, I relished, yes relished (don't be so shocked that I possess a vocabulary that goes beyond four-letter expletives and animal sounds) my reputation as an American hero—me and Lucky Lindy, icons of the golden Twenties (although what happened to him after Hauptman kidnapped his kid—well that's another story). Yes, my father put me in an orphan's home and sure, as any of those books will tell you, some of my flamboyance and desire for attention was payback for what I didn't get from my old man. But what do you really know about my internal struggles, my contemplative side, my private thoughts and personal emotions that make up the substance of any human being? Surprised again? The Babe stringing together complicated thoughts and ideas, implicitly critiquing books and films along the way? Even as dilettante, an unexpected achievement, doubly so from someone dead for more than fifty years.

So, in honor of my birthday and as balance to public depictions of my life, past, present, and future, I give you *The Rabbi of Swat*. Actually, Peter Levine gives it to you. Or so he thinks. But as you'll see, without him knowing it, I've intruded to serve my own needs. So read about Morrie Ginsberg and enjoy the tale. Just don't forget the driving force behind it.

BABE RUTH HE WASN'T. Not a chance he'd be mistaken for the slicked-back, black-haired Yankee Strong Man—a contradiction of lithe muscle and midwaist fat on a 220 lb., 6'2" frame—baseball's biggest man in every way. Six inches shorter, all skin and bone—curly brown hair and a large bent nose—Morrie Ginsberg didn't care; even if the papers already were poking fun at John McGraw's latest experiment to outdraw the Great Bambino. So proclaimed the *World's* Mike McConnell: "The Rabbi of Swat doesn't stand a chance against the Sultan of Swat, not at the box office and never face to face,"— the lead line on his story that Jake read to his son over breakfast in the kitchen at 737 Sackman Street.

"Let McConnell have his fun. It sells newspapers. The fact is I'm on the train to the Polo Grounds today to play against the Pirates— not bad for a nice Jewish boy from Brownsville, huh, Pa?"

Jake grunted incomprehensible acknowledgement—more often than not what passed for conversation between father and son—

his eyes focused on the paper, his lips occupied with a sugar cube through which he sucked his tea in the yahrzeit glass in front of him. Such a practical country—memorial candles for the dead in reusable drinking glasses. No such thing in the Russian shtetl he had left over twenty years ago to come to America to escape the pogroms and avoid getting killed in the Tsar's war against Japan.

No baseball there either. Or stoop ball, stick ball, or punch ball. Streets there took young boys to work or to cheder. Here they doubled as baseball diamonds and football fields. Streetlights became baskets and sewers outfield fences.

This much Jake understood. Occasionally, when Morrie was younger he helped him wrap up old socks and rags into a makeshift ball. Once, for his birthday, he even bought him his own pink rubber ball the kids called spaldeens. He didn't even get upset when Morrie and his friends dug holes in the small dirt patch next to the front stoop that passed as their front yard and played golf with their bats and balls. When Morrie played basketball for the evening recreation center and baseball at Boys High, Jake sometimes went to see him play. After all this was Brooklyn in America—a place, if not for himself then at least for his son, that offered a better, safer life than any Russian childhood he might have experienced. Not even in the wildest parts of his imagination, however, did he ever dream that his own flesh and blood would end up playing a child's game for a living.

Mama had less trouble. Although Jake was her husband, Morrie was her pride. Baseball she knew from nothing. But love and loyalty to her own came from the heart. Sometimes it wasn't so easy—to be proud of Morrie without hurting Jake or to love her husband without excluding her boy required a delicate touch that she blundered more often than not, unconsciously meting out indiscriminate punishment on one or the other as situations arose. Today, however, belonged to Morrie. She knew it, he knew it, and Jake, enveloped in his tea and his paper, knew it too.

———————————

———

Jake rarely left Brooklyn. Once or twice a year they went to the Bronx to visit Mama's cousin from Smolensk, and then only reluctantly. He hated the elevated—the crush of people, the looks and smells of others who were not his kind—"melting pot, shmelting pot," he complained to Mama whenever they left the familiar world of Sackman Street. True, he didn't go to shul very often but Mama kept kosher and always lit the Friday night candles. But every time he stepped out of his house, he knew who he was and where he came from. The candy store where he bought his cigars on his way to work sold more copies of the *Jewish Daily Forward* than it did the *New York World*; the fruit stall, butcher, bakery, and fish stores all displayed their merchandise under banners in Hebrew letters proclaiming the virtues and prices of their stock while their owners, many with yarmulkes on their heads and their tzitzit hanging over their belts— on floors strewn with sawdust—engaged their customers in Yiddish chatter. Here no one was a stranger. The streets smelled of his past and defined his present—the names on the mailboxes and the faces in the windows on hot summer days like this one—no matter what he was thinking or feeling inside—always told him he was home.

Today, however, he was going to the Polo Grounds at Coogan's Bluff. It would be hot, but Mama insisted he get dressed up, like it was Morrie's bar mitzvah all over again. Putting on his woolen, blue suit, he entertained incongruous visions of rich, Manhattan goyim riding horses and swinging mallets on some land owned by a drunken Irishman. His own acquaintance with horses involved sturdier breeds that pulled plows and milk carts on the dirt streets of his Russian boyhood or the wares of street merchants on the Lower East Side where he lived when he first came to America.

He thought of sharing his imagination with Esther—Mama, he called her, when he and Morrie were both around her—Esther, when she seemed there for him alone, but she was too busy stuffing a basket with lunch to listen.

"Jake, give me a tomato from the window," she barked. "You'll like it with the hard-boiled eggs and herring sandwiches we'll take."

"Yes, Mama," he sighed, wiping the soot off an overly ripe one that had sat on the ledge one day too long. Even if he had told her, she wouldn't have understood how clever he had been. To her, polo was a shirt not a game. It wouldn't have been worth the trouble to explain the difference. Besides, as he already knew, although the food she was packing was for him, her head was full of Morrie.

Morrie stood on the platform as the train pulled out of the elevated station, leaving him a view of the Polo Grounds and the Harlem River coursing below it. On its murky, dirty surface he could see Columbia College boys rowing their thin, spider-like boats across the water. Across it, only a few blocks up from the Polo Grounds, loomed Yankee Stadium, "The House that Ruth Built" and packed along with the rest of Murderer's Row, as the sportswriters fondly called the invincible men in pinstripes.

Morrie had been there before. Not to the Polo Grounds but to the Bronx Jewish Community Center across the Grand Concourse when he and the Dux came to play basketball against its varsity five. Major travel for the Dux then, he recalled—Sammy, Dudie, Jammy, Nat, Whitey, Burtie and Morrie—veterans of Nanny Goat Park and the evening recreation center at P.S. 184 where they won the Brooklyn championship their last year of junior high school—named the Dux because Sammy's older brother who was in high school when they formed the club, told them that Dux meant "leader" in Latin. "Besides, it's short," he reminded them, requiring only three pink felt letters for their team jackets—black satin jobs bought at discount at Modell's, $5.00 each, money earned in the early evening hawking newspapers, gum and candy at corners and subway kiosks, confronting people as they hurried home from work with sensational headlines and penny treats in chase of dimes and nickels.

Mama sewed them on while Jake watched. "Put the money away for something important," he reminded his son. "Why waste it on a jacket that will end up with the junk man or in the closet?"

"You don't understand, Pa. This is important to me."

"You're right. I don't understand. You spend all this time with balls and your friends when you should be saving and thinking about your future."

But it was precisely in places like the Bronx JCC where his future took hold. "The city's alive for us, Ginnzie," Burtie proclaimed that first night on the Grand Concourse as the Dux, surrounded by admirers, flush with victory and their share of the gate, headed for Times Square for a late dinner and show.

Sweaty excitement, the sense of possibility, of breaking away from the familiar, of being somebody other than "Jake and Esther's boy," of being "alive" to the world outside Sackman Street, the noisy adulation of friends and strangers who applauded his physical talents, the chance to travel to new places, even as far as Hartford and Springfield to play other center and Y teams, doing something he was good at that pleased other people and even occasionally getting paid a few dollars—was lure enough. And baseball was his game.

That is what he tried to tell Jake the night Harold Leary, the New York Giants' chief scout came to the house on Sackman Street only three days after he graduated from high school to offer him a spot on the Giants' Tuscaloosa, Alabama Class B farm team. Sure, Alabama was not the Bronx, but the unknown was familiar enough; the risks more enticing than frightening.

"That's what they teach us in school. You always tell me to put my education to use, well I am!" But Jake didn't understand.

"You risked life and limb to come to America, Pa. And now you're afraid to leave the block! Well, I'm not you. You can't make me into what I'm not!"

"And what are you? A bum who spends all his time in that park—all the time with the balls. Is this what I work so hard for, so you can go away and waste your time with these farshtinkener games?"

"A waste of time! I'll make more in a month than you make in two and have a good time doing it. Isn't that enough for you?"

"But the future, Morrie, think of the future. . . ."

Such words between father and son! Such words to the father who held a son's future in his hands! Although a man by Jewish law since his bar mitzvah, Morrie was still a minor four years later, according to the state of New York, requiring his father's signature on the unsigned Giants contract that Leary explained to the entire family over the kitchen table: "A $200 bonus for signing and $50.00 a month plus expenses while your boy gets a taste of the game in Tuscaloosa. And we'll make sure he writes home every week, Mrs. Ginsberg," Leary laughed, "don't you worry."

"Sign, Jake, sign," his mother finally spoke. "It has to be Moey's choice."

And he did, without another word.

"You won't regret this, Mr. Ginsberg," Harold Leary assured Jake as he shook his reluctant hand. "Your boy here has a fine arm and a solid future with us." Jake looked away—his face marked by that combination of disgust and disappointment so familiar to confrontations between father and son. And Morrie's face, angry and embarrassed at the same time. . . .

———————

———

The clang of metal wheels on rails announced the arrival of still another car filled with eager Giants' rooters, separating Morrie from his memories and propelling him down the stairs, through the turnstiles and onto a street already crowded with vendors selling pennants, pretzels, and hot dogs to the early arrivals. No one recognized him as he walked around the park to the players' entrance even though the *World* had carried an old picture of him in his Syracuse Chief's outfit with a caption announcing the late-season arrival of a new "Hebrew" star, alongside McConnell's column. Even the groundskeeper had to call into the clubhouse to see if one Morrie Ginsberg, whose face he did not recognize and whose name was not on the gate list, was really playing for the Giants today. John McGraw assured him he was.

McGraw had kept his eye on Morrie all year. The kid had impressed him in Sarasota that March. He was only 20, the same age Mathewson had been when he came up to the club. He didn't have the overpowering stuff that Matty had. They sure didn't look alike. And this Jewish kid was not a college boy like Christy. But he knew the game, was a quick learner, and played with a zest and enthusiasm that reminded him of his protégé and friend, who had died that past fall.

There was even a trace of himself in this young kid. Not in appearance certainly. Overweight now at 220 lbs, his 5' 7" frame constantly torn from clogged sinuses and allergies that swelled his face and commanded a steady flow of snot and mucous from his nostrils—dressed in a white linen suit, tie, silk Cuban shirt, and straw hat—even McGraw sometimes had trouble remembering himself as the lithe, fiery ballplayer who, with his pal Huey Jennings, had led the Baltimore Orioles to pennants and championships in the 1890s. But watching Morrie in spring training taking his turns in the batting cage and bearing down with each pitch, rekindled those feelings of intensity and determination that had made him the most combative player on one of the game's most contentious teams. It wasn't for nothing that he had earned the nickname Muggsy, although it had been years since anybody called him that.

He almost brought Morrie east in April. The pressure was there. After a run of four consecutive pennants—three memorable World Series clashes with the Yankees and even two championships in 1921 and 1922—the club had faltered. Injuries and his own illness had taken their toll. The Giants had dropped to fifth place—their worst showing since finishing last in 1915. Nor had things been too good at the gate since Ruth moved in across the river.

"Bring up the Jew boy," Horace Stoneham, the Giants' chief stockholder, urged. "He'll be worth his weight in gold whether he can play or not."

But Mac resisted. He wasn't Little Napoleon for nothing. Although he didn't own as much of the club as Stoneham, the Giants were his team—had been since he came over from Baltimore in 1902. He called all the shots, set the strategy, made decisions about who played where and when; even told the pitchers what to throw.

And it had worked. The magic had returned. The club started slowly, fell behind the Pirates and Cubs early, even trailed the "trolley" Dodgers from Brooklyn until well into June. But here it was the last week in August and the club was only five games behind Pittsburgh. He had been right to wait until now. Ginsberg had matured upstate. He had put together a nice change-up to go along with his curve so even his fast ball seemed quicker than it was. And the kid could hit. The Chiefs even used him as a pinch hitter and several times in right-field just for his bat.

"Maybe he will be worth his weight in gold," thought McGraw, as he finished pencilling in Morrie's name as pitcher and last in the batting order on his lineup card, puffing on the cigar that hung out of the side of his mouth—but not only because of his name and his nose."

Morrie's knock on the manager's door brought Mac face to face with his new starting pitcher and Morrie with baseball legend.

"Mr. McGraw? I'm Morrie. . . .

"Hey young man, glad to see you here. I've had my eye on you since training camp. I think you can help us down the stretch. You just listen to me and pay attention. Come on, let me show you around."

Straightforward and to the point this John McGraw, just like Hal Woodhouse, the Chiefs' manager had advised him when he told Morrie that the big club wanted him in New York. "This is your chance Morrie, don't blow it. The bats come around faster, the crowds are bigger, but the game is still the same. Remember that."

Well at least the clubhouse wasn't much different, Morrie thought, taking in the shabby confines of the locker room—peeling paint and iron mesh cubby holes for your clothes, as Mr. McGraw—all the players called him that—introduced him to some of the Giant regulars and then sat him down with Zack Taylor to go over the Pirates' line-up.

"Don't worry about anything but getting the ball into Zack's mitt," McGraw instructed. "I'll signal him what pitch to call and he'll let you know."

"These guys don't hit the long ball but they're pesky—especially Traynor and the Waners," added Taylor. "Just watch my fingers for the sign and my glove for the spot and we'll be Okee Dokee," he continued, flashing the gnarled and battered tools of his trade, as if to reassure Morrie that everything was in good hands.

Morrie hoped so. Not that he doubted his arm—but this was the Polo Grounds—the papers anticipated a crowd of 30,000 fans, the Giants were still in the hunt for the pennant, and his parents would be somewhere in the grandstand. He found his cubicle just where the clubhouse boy told him it would be ("the last one on the right next to the john,") sat down on a stool and began unpacking the paper bag that contained a fresh change of underwear, his leather glove, and his shoes. "Maybe a little prayer to God wouldn't hurt," he mused. "Who knows? Maybe he's a baseball fan too."

JAKE MUSED TOO. Not about God's interest in the Giants but
about the day. At every stop on the trek from Brooklyn to the Polo
Grounds, especially as the train pushed through the Lower East Side
and the garment district, the doors opened to engulf his mish-
pocheh. Or so it seemed. Jewish men and boys, even a few women,
dressed in their best like he and Mama, pushed in and filled the cars
until they were as crowded and familiar as the steerage of the boat
that brought him to America. By the time the train reached 96th
Street it reeked familiar—the smells from countless lunch baskets
intermingled in the dank, humid air—as if a kosher appetizing store
full of herring, pickles, chopped liver and shmaltz had packed itself
along for the occasion. And the occasion was clear. Tailors, cutters,
pushkies, shoemakers—old and young—jabbering to each other in
Yiddish and English, all proclaiming the same reason for their
exuberant mood; they were all on their way to watch his son play
baseball.

They all sat together in the lower right-field stands. Not that they had to. Fifty cents general admission entitled you to any chair in the vast double-decked grandstand that embraced the newly renovated ballpark. So Jake learned from one of his new companions, a Jewish man only a few years younger than himself, who announced, to no one in particular, all that he knew about the Polo Grounds and his beloved Giants as Jake and Esther, along with their trainload of landsmen, disembarked on the same station platform that Morrie had left only a few hours before.

Pushed along by the crowd, by the time Jake and Esther made it to their seats, they heard that the Giants had spent over $400,000 to rebuild the park, doing away with the old wooden bleachers, eliminating the spot in center field where wealthy folk came in their carriages to take in an inning or two, and adding a grandstand that swept out from home plate to flank a four-story building in center-field that housed dressing rooms and club offices. "Can you believe it?" their tour guide exclaimed, "all this just to attract you and me from the Babe's Yankees to McGraw's Giants!"

Free to sit wherever they chose, more than their own momentum led Jake, Esther, and the others to their place in right field. The same common bond that Jake had felt with the people of his streets drew them together. Some knew their baseball and enjoyed it as sport. Most, however, were there less as aficionados than as proud and nervous members of an extended family, rambunctious in their happiness that one of their own was on public display for all to see and anxious that he do well—the bar mitzvah ritual extended to a goyish world by an American "invention."

Surrounded by his own, engulfed by the excitement of the talk around him—"Ginsberg can do it," "Morrie—such a boy—

from Brownsville—Nu—a rabbi's son?"—Jake said nothing. Mama beamed, peeled him an egg, had no idea what she was about to see, didn't understand who this Babe was, and couldn't have cared less. Her boy was everybody's son; his name on everyone's lips. Taking the tomato from the basket, she bit into its juicy flesh and turned to hand it to Jake. Unfortunate timing, for the Giants picked that very moment to rush out of their dugout along the first-base line and run out onto the field. People erupted in cheers and shouts around her. The man next to her jumped up so fast that his right arm jostled her elbow and sent the tomato splattering on the concrete.

"There he is, there's Ginsberg," he and the others shouted as the young pitcher walked slowly out to the mound.

Mama didn't understand. Morrie was so far away that it was hard to be sure that the man standing on a little brown hill surrounded by green grass marked with white lines and squares of white cloth was her son. Of course she knew that Morrie played baseball for a living. She knew too well how Jake felt about it. But no one, not even Morrie on that horrible night when that Mr. Leary came to the house, had ever explained it to her. Right now, she wished she knew more. What were these other men, also with the same silly caps on their heads that Morrie had on, doing on the hill that her son had run out to? And what about the man walking towards them holding a stick in his hand? Both she and her son were about to find out.

―――――――――
―――

While Jake explained to Mama, Zack handed Morrie the Spalding, went over the signs, patted him on his behind, and returned to home plate. Morrie stepped off the mound and turned to the center-field clubhouse, all the while rubbing the ball with both hands, the sound and feel of skin squeezing on leather; ritual beginning for any ball game—familiar and comforting—whether on city streets or major league diamonds.

"Don't be nervous boy," confident advice from Rogers Hornsby, Giants' second baseman and captain—so McGraw said when the twelve-year St. Louis veteran joined the club in the off-season—who interrupted Morrie's reverie, took the ball from his hands and pounded it into the pocket of his own glove. Traded for Johnny Ring and Frankie Frisch, the "Fordham Flash," Rajah, who had just led the Crescent City club, as player and manager, to its first World Series victory—over the Yankees no less—had not been so sure of his place in April. Angry fans and sportswriters eager for controversy let McGraw know that they missed their New York boy; their Queens-born Bronx hero who played baseball in Manhattan. Resentful teammates wondered out loud if Hornsby was worth the $40,000 Stoneham shelled out for his services. But Hornsby did his job, both at the plate and as captain, sometimes filling in for McGraw as field general when the old man's sinus attacks made it too difficult for him to come to the park. Now, with the Giants surging and each game on the line, Rajah played his part.

"Steaks and pie á la mode on me after the game. Remember, just put it over the plate and we'll take care of the rest."

Morrie nodded, caught the ball that his captain tossed to him as he headed back to his position between first and second base, and turned to look in at Lloyd Waner, the Pirates rookie lead-off man and center fielder. Although the legendary second baseman could not have known it, the thought of his promised unholy alliance churning around in the young pitcher's stomach tightened the knots already in place since Morrie first took the field. Ever since he was a kid, he always had trouble with stomachs, not only his own. Once, in third grade, he asked his teacher, one Mrs. Hogan of P.S. 184, if Jews had two stomachs like cows—one milchedig for dairy and one flayshedig for meat. That problem he solved, but his own could still give him trouble.

Waner had been an unexpected surprise for the Pirates. He started the year in left field when the Bucs' regular there, Clyde Barnhart, reported to camp weighing in at over 240 pounds. By the time the Butterball had rounded into shape and resumed his duties, "Little Poison," as Lloyd became known, had found a regular berth in center. True to form, he lashed Morrie's first pitch, a hanging curve that never made it to his fists, over Hornsby's head into right field.

Morrie heard both the moans from the right-field stands and the taunts from the Pirate dugout as he waited for Pie Traynor to step in. This time, however, his curve found the corners and the third baseman went down on four pitches. Paul Waner, "Big Poison," who outweighed his brother by twenty pounds on the same 5'9" frame, was another story. Morrie battled the right fielder as he fouled off five pitches in a row before drawing a walk. Two Waners on, one out, and Butterball at the plate.

Zack Taylor called time and joined his pitcher. "Take your time, don't rush the ball," he cautioned. "He's a sucker for a slow pitch. Lob it up there like a grapefruit, and this Florida boy will guarantee you that he'll chop it into the ground for an easy double play. This klutz can't run at all."

Morrie almost fell off the mound. Only with the Dux and in the streets had he heard such talk from teammates. Were there Jews in

Florida? Even if, not Zack, Morrie concluded, as Tom McGinty, the home-plate umpire, motioned the catcher back to home plate. Relaxed for the first time since he stepped onto the field, Morrie tantalized Barnhart with a slow curve that he hit weakly to Bill Terry at first. Terry charged the grounder, fired over to Jackson at second who returned a quick throw to Morrie covering the base a good three steps before Barnhart crossed the bag.

At least this time Jake managed to swallow the last of his hard-boiled egg before the more vociferous baseball fans around him pounded each other on their backs and screamed approval of their Jewish Giant. Others, like Mama, who didn't know the difference between a double play and a twin bill at the movie house on Pitkin Avenue, nevertheless joined in the chorous of "gevalts," "atta boy's," and "mechaiehs"—a joyous cacophony of Yiddish and American sounds in praise of her boy that quieted to a murmur of pride and pointing when she stood up, turned around to her neighbors and announced to them that their cheers were for her boy. Jake kept his seat, said nothing, and offered only an embarrassed smile when the man next to him admiringly shook his hand.

And so it went. No more spectacular plays for Morrie but a solid outing with the rock. The Bucs did pick up two runs in the fourth when Johnny Gooch doubled and came in on Joe Harris's home run to right. But Morrie stifled the Pirates through the seventh and Bill Terry, the Giants' first sacker, got one run back in the bottom of the fifth with a tremendous home run to left field.

Morrie had less success at the plate. Specs Hill, the Pirates' ace righthander—a fast-ball pitcher who appeared especially dangerous as he peered through his milk bottle glasses to get his signs—threw him out at first on a tap back to the mound in the second and struck him out on three pitches in the fifth. Although hardly as intimidating a figure on the mound, Morrie returned the favor in the top of the seventh to end the inning.

Freddie Lindstrom opened the Giants' half by flying out to Big Poison in left. Bill Terry could do no better, popping up to short. Eddie Roush fell behind 0–2 to Hill's fast balls but then reached out for a curve and chopped it through the hole between first and second into right for a single. Then Doc Farrell dragged a bunt down third for a hit—first and third, two outs, time for McGraw to make his move.

Morrie figured his day was done as soon as he struck out Hill. He had pitched a solid seven innings but the Giants still trailed and he was due up fourth in their half. If anyone got on, no way would he be allowed to bat. On one knee in the on-deck circle, he watched Reese scramble down the line in front of the Giants' dugout. As Andy crossed the bag, Morrie stood up and started walking towards the dugout, both disappointed and relieved at the prospect of being pulled for a pinch hitter. McGraw, watching from his usual place at the end of the Giant bench, entertained similar thoughts. Baseball logic dictated it. Besides he had another rookie fresh up from the minors named Ott, who he was eager to try. But hunches, at the racetrack or the ballpark, were always part of his game. Moving to the front of the dugout steps, he looked up at his startled young pitcher: "Take your time up there, It's your game to win or lose."

Shouts of "Jew boy," "kike" and other obscenities flew out at Morrie from the Pirates' dugout, counterpoint to the encouraging sounds that floated in from the right-field stands. Settling into the box, he turned towards Hill, determined to swing at the first pitch anywheres near the strike zone.

And it was. The Pirates' pitcher challenged him with a fast ball and true to his vow, the Rabbi of Swat lashed it into left field, chasing Waner all the way to the wall. By the time he made it to second, two runs had scored and the Giants led 3 to 2. Morrie managed to shut out the Pirates the rest of the way and Zack Taylor added an insurance home run in the bottom of the eighth. When it was all over, the Giants won 4 to 2, McGraw was all smiles, and Morrie's Jewish constituency had made the ballpark ring in ways that neither Mr. Coogan nor his polo players could have ever imagined.

After Morrie's double, his self-appointed fans lost all control. The enthusiasm and pride that had filled the grandstand when Jake and Mama's son took the mound in the first inning was no match for the craziness that followed his feat at the plate. Ignoring the sweltering late-August sun that bathed them in heat and perspiration, sweaty men and women hugged each other, danced in the aisles and sang Morrie's praise to the heavens. Many took turns crowding around his parents, congratulating them for having produced such a fine boy. By the top of the ninth, no one was sitting. Shouting and cheering every curve and change-up Morrie delivered, they erupted when Pie Traynor grounded out to Terry to end the game.

Even Mama, who, that afternoon, made little progress toward understanding even the difference between three strikes and four balls, recognized that baseball games didn't usually end the way this one did. While she and Jake watched, boys and men climbed over the right-field fence and headed towards second base as Morrie left the mound and ran, along with the Pirates and the rest of his Giant teammates, towards the center-field clubhouse. Like slaves fleeing the Pharaoh or the locusts who had plagued their oppressors, a fury of Jewish soldiers surged towards their Moses and engulfed him. Hoisted on their shoulders, Morrie was carried around the Polo Grounds amidst joyous voices shouting his name—both groom and bride at once, aloft in their chairs, in celebration of a new life.

Morrie felt more like an Egyptian swallowed by the Red Sea. Never was a Jewish boy more grateful to see a pack of goyim, dressed in Giant uniforms, churn through the crowd, pluck him from his perch, part the "sea" with a flying wedge and carry him to the safety of the center-field steps.

AS ALWAYS, JAKE AROSE first and shuffled to the door for the *World.* Today he had slept a little longer than usual. It was already 6:30. Morrie's celebration had kept him up well past his normal bedtime and the gas from the delicatessen much of the night.

A man of routines, yesterday had shaken him. Mama's escort to Morrie's day, he, too, found himself caught up in the frenzy of the moment. True, he hadn't danced in the aisles or charged onto the field. But watching his boy carried aloft and accepting congratulations from his new friends in the grandstand left him unsettled.

When they arrived back on Sackman Street, Mama fussed over Morrie and the neighbors toasted his son with holiday wine brought out to mark the occasion, packing the second floor railroad flat they rented. Jake never moved from the kitchen table, retreating behind a mask of cigar smoke and his glass of tea. Bering Plazas, five cents a piece, his daily pleasure, now plucked one at a time from the wooden cigar box he kept in a bedroom dresser drawer, once purchased one at a time for him every day at Steinberg's candy store around the corner by Morrie, who patiently used to wait while his father carefully peeled the cellophane wrapper and removed the gold and red paper ring without damaging the cigar's rolled leaves, and then placing it delicately on Morrie's middle finger.

No rings today, however. Not for a long time. Rings and cigars foregone, opportunities squandered to make things better between them. That's what had shaken Jake. Not in so many words but in the empty feeling that troubled him as much as the cramps he carried over from the night before.

Morrie pretended not to notice. He, too, knew how to mask what he felt about his father, more often with anger and sarcasm than with silence. Shuffling back and forth from one group of well-wishers to another—well-intentioned neighbors, his cousins from Pitkin Avenue who knew as much about baseball as his mother, even Burtie and Sammy and their girlfriends—all packed together in August humid swelter; amidst backslappings, handshakes, silently beaming faces, and huzzahs—suffocating celebration that left him gasping for air at open windows in the windless night—Morrie too felt empty. And angry. Not just at Jake but at himself. For not being elsewhere, anywhere, maybe eating steak and ice cream with Hornsby, maybe . . . anywhere but Sackman Street.

Jake's breakfast reading didn't help; McConnell's column, a poem actually, "Ginsberg at the Bat," neatly arranged as border to a large photo of Morrie at the plate under a headline that read BROWNSVILLE BOYCHIK BRINGS HOME THE BACON.

"Listen to this," he bellowed, as Morrie and Mama descended on the kitchen table where he sat with his morning tea. "Look what you look like for all the world to see." Jake read out loud:

———————————

———

The outlook wasn't cheerful for the Giants yesterday,

They were trailing by a run with but three innings left to play.

When Lindstrom flied to Waner and Terry weakly popped,

It looked as though those Pirates had the game as good as copped.

But Roush chopped a single over Glenn Wright's pate,

And Reese followed with another, bunting smartly at the plate.

And from the stands and bleachers the cry of "Oy, Oy" rose,

And up came Morrie Ginsberg, half a foot behind his nose.

There was ease in Specs Hill's manner and a smile on Traynor's face,

For they figured they had Morrie in the tightest sort of place.

It was make or break for Morrie while the fans cried, "Oy, Oy, Oy."

And it wasn't any soft spot for a little Jewish boy.

And now the pitcher has the ball and now he lets it go.

And now the air is shattered by the force of Casey's blow.

Well nothing like that happened, but what do you suppose?

Why little Morrie Ginsberg socked the ball upon the nose.

Then from the stands and bleachers the fans in triumph roared,

And Morrie raced to second and the other runners scored.

Soon they took him home in triumph amidst the blare of auto honks.

There may be no joy in Mudville but there's plenty in the Bronx.

———————————

———

"So what's so terrible, Jake?" Mama asked. "It's special to see Moey's name and picture in the paper, nu?"

"Nu? Don't you listen? He makes fun of Morrie, of all of us—how we talk, our size, what we look like—weak, puny greenhorns play-ing where they don't belong. At least that part he has right."

"What are you so upset about? My big nose? So the man's an anti-Semite bastard! Is this the first one you've met? Who cares! At least he recognizes who I am and what I mean to people."

"And what is that? You play a stupid game, a job for bums not men, and this makes you important? Such a country I don't under-stand!"

"Jake, please!"

"A bum I am? And maybe bums don't live here? Not on wonder-ful Sackman Street! What would the neighbors say!"

"Suit yourself!"

With that, Jake pushed himself away from the table, slammed down the paper and headed down the hall to the bathroom. Con-versation closed—typical interchange between father and son, punctuated as always by Mama's admonishments and amends:

"You shouldn't talk to your father that way; he really loves you or does love you"—the choice of words depending upon how charged the confrontation had been that she had witnessed.

This one, Mama knew, had been serious. Mudville and Casey were lost on her but she understood how much Jake had hurt Morrie.

"He really does love you, Morrie," she pleaded weakly, waiting for her son to give her the usual quizzical look or wisecrack before moving on to other things. This time, however, the Giants' rising star, yesterday's hero, the Moses of the Bronx, said nothing. Instead, he sat down in his father's chair, smoothed out the crumpled page con-taining McConnell's poem, and began to read it to himself. This time it did not make him laugh. By the time he "socked the ball on the nose," "little Morrie Ginsberg" was in tears, his head down on the table, cradled in his mother's arms, as she comforted him with "sha's" and yiddish murmurings that he had heard since he could remember.

THE BABE AWOKE to different sounds—the clamoring noise of city streets outside his hotel window on West 72nd Street and the knock on his door announcing the arrival of room service and the beginning of another day for the Sultan of Swat.

Putting on his red velvet robe and matching Morrocan slippers, baseball's most famous player picked his way over beer bottles and plates of unfinished food—the remnants of last night's party—and let the bellhop in with his breakfast, morning paper, and sodium bicarbonate.

"Put it near the window keed, I'll take care of you later," he croaked, an unnecessary comment to any of the regular staff at the Alamac who knew the Babe's routine and who could count on a handsome tip for their service and discretion.

Babe downed the bicarbonate crystals even before the bellhop left, hoping for immediate relief from the indigestion and hangover that seemed his constant companions each morning. Today was a bit worse than usual. Last night's hoopla celebrating the opening of "The Babe Comes Home" began in the limousine that swept down the west side from the Roxy on 42nd Street to Delmonico's at the tip of Manhattan and didn't end until four in the morning when the last of his well-wishers cleared out of his hotel suite.

Undeterred for long by the state of his stomach, Babe began his daily assault on the morning paper and a mountainous breakfast of wheatcakes and ham, combination and quantity that had become standard morning fare ever since he first signed with Baltimore in 1913 and learned that his meals were on the club.

Halfway through both, he found the *World*'s review of his movie debut—Babe Ruth as Babe Dugan, a tobacco-chewing ballplayer for the Los Angeles Angels who gives up his nasty habit for the love of a laundry girl, falls into a slump without the magical powers of nicotine, and returns to it in time to win both the pennant and his lady in the bottom of the ninth. As the *World* turned, all those months on the Pantages vaudeville circuit reciting poetry, singing songs, and signing autographs for $5,000 a week, had not made the Babe an actor. "When it comes to acting," he read, "he's is in the same class with the Prince of Wales in a jockey role. Babe may make home runs but he was never built for romance under the kliegs."

"Shit, at least they got the story right," he groaned, quickly turning to the sports page, expecting solace in the usual attention accorded him there. After all, yesterday he had hit his 43rd home run for a team that had long since buried the competition in its quest for a fifth pennant since he had come to the Yankees in 1920. Why only last night, his ever-vigilant confidant and publicity agent Christy Walsh reminded him of the potential gold mine if he should surpass the 59 round-trippers he hit in 1921.

Instead, he discovered the Rabbi of Swat center page; the account of his own exploits relegated to a sidebar. Hardly an avid or careful reader of anything, the Bambino scanned "Ginsberg at the Bat" focusing instead on Morrie's large picture and the caption that summarized the accomplishments of the "hawk-nosed" pitcher who had tamed the Pirates with his pitching and his bat.

"Son of a bitch," he chuckled to himself as he tossed the paper to the floor and headed into the bathroom. "Sounds like a description of me when I first came up—a good hitting pitcher with 'niggerlips' instead of a schnozz." Never much for nostalgia, the Babe left Morrie and his own past behind as he turned on the shower and prepared himself for another day's work at the house he built.

Actually Eddie Barrow and Jacob Ruppert, general manager and owner of the New York Yankees, built the Babe's house, but to his specifications and dimensions. Even larger than the Polo Grounds where the Yankees played for several seasons while their own ballpark was under construction, Yankee Stadium seated 62,000, with a triple-decked grandstand, complete with an ornate concrete curly-cued facade extending beyond the left-field foul pole and bleachers that swept across the outfield. Above the bleachers, a huge center-field scoreboard kept track of all major league games inning by inning. A short right-field fence accommodated Babe's propensity to hit home runs down the line. And with him in the line-up, it turned out to be a bargain at $2,500,000.

Outside its gates, across the Grand Concourse and down 161st Street, fans, foodsellers, scalpers, and barkers milled around in a festive spirit, awaiting their opening and the onset of the Yankees' Labor Day clash with the Detroit Tigers. Especially noticeable was the crowd of young boys at the players' entrance. Pockets of them surged briefly as Tony Lazzeri, the Yankees' Italian rookie shortstop and Waite Hoyt, the "Flatbush Mortician," nicknamed by Brooklyn birth and father's occupation, came to work. They cheered more loudly and clustered in greater numbers when Columbia Lou Gehrig, only one home run behind Ruth, arrived from his mother's home in the Bronx. But the real target of their vigil was the Babe. No matter how many of them there were, no matter what the weather or the time, he never disappointed them. He answered their questions, signed their scorecards, shook their hands, and handed out candy bars, even Baby Ruths, despite the fact that they had more to do with Herbert Hoover's granddaughter than himself.

Today was no exception. Babe's "train," a chauffeur-driven red Packard limousine hired especially for him by the club as much for his ego as to protect him from the adoring "flocks of femninity," as one scribe called them, pulled up by the curb and deposited him amidst his young fans.

"Hello keeds, how are you," the Babe bellowed to his fans.

Candy bars flew in all directions, hands reached out to touch him, questions and requests filled his ears as the Yankee Hero, the Mauling Monarch, George Herman Ruth signed his name and best wishes on every scrap of paper thrust at him.

The Yankee giant savored it all. His own childhood had left little time for hero worship or candy bars; his treats came from quick fingers at candy store counters, not from doting parents or baseball heroes. Placed in a Baltimore orphan's home by his father, his namesake and itinerant saloon keeper. . . .

[Whoa! Slow down boy! Loosen up. First of all everybody knows this litany, how my father put me in St. Mary's Orphan's home, how I spent ten years there, how Brother Matthias and Brother George taught me about God, shirt-making, and baseball, especially baseball, how I left as a man to sign with Baltimore and so on. And for Christ's sake, remember you're not writing a textbook. Keep it flowing, let the story unfold, the characters take shape.]

But he never forgot what he missed growing up and offered it freely to the loyal following of young boys who repaid him with the attention he never tired of. Of all his insatiable appetites, this one was most important.

———————

The Tigers paid attention too. They had no choice. "C'mon Jidge, Let's have at 'em, boy!" Miller Huggins, the Yankees' manager, shouted to Ruth, as Eddie Bennett, the hunchbacked bat boy handed Babe his lumber as he headed towards the plate. Bottom of the first and already Detroit knew it was in for a long day. Earl Combs led off with a single, Mark "Anthony" Koenig sacrificed him to second and Gehrig walked, setting the table for the Sultan of Swat.

Larry Woodhall called time and trotted out from behind the plate to settle down Haskell Billings, the Tigers' nineteen-year-old righthander just up from Toledo. Although the air was cool, Billings was sweating badly—not the good smell of athletic exertion but the stench of nervous exhaustion brought on by the prospect of annihilation at the hands of the Yankee slugger. "Don't be afraid, boy," Woodhall told his charge. "Just keep it outside—nothing too good to hit. You could do a lot worse than walk him."

Billings nodded, too terrified by the prospect of facing Ruth yet strangely exhilarated by the thrill of it all.

Babe didn't bother to acknowledge his first pitch which caught the outside corner for a strike. Instead he stepped out of the box and roamed the ballpark with his eyes and ears; taking in the large holiday crowd and the patriotic bunting that covered the lower deck stands and the grandstand façade; listening, as gentlemen in the $2.00 boxes and young boys empowered by their fifty-cent bleacher seats, shouted his name and clamored for their hero to deliver what they had come to see.

Focused on Billings for the first time, Ruth stepped back in and watched the next pitch for a ball. Then he settled in for the curve he expected on the outside corner.

Billings delivered as scheduled and so did the Babe. With all the strength his massive 220-pound frame could manage, he whirled at the ball with such power that a miss threatened to screw him into the ground by the force of his own momentum. Fortunately for the Babe and for the thousands who had come to see him, for the 44th time since April 7th, he didn't. Before you could say Ty Cobb, the ball ended up a couple of dozen rows into the second deck of the right-field stands. Charlie Gehringer, the Tigers' feisty second baseman, kicked the ground in disgust as he watched the Babe trot by in his familiar short-stepped home run gait while the crowd managed a roar even louder than the one that had first greeted their hero as he stepped up to hit.

"You're down two, Lou," Ruth joked with Gehrig as the Yankee first baseman shook his hand at homeplate. Odd fellows, the pair. As explosive, flamboyant, and unpredictable as Ruth was, his teammate and home-run challenger was quiet, unassuming, and routine. Eight years apart in age and further separated in other ways, nevertheless they got along fine as teammates. Together, they made great copy for the wire services and the press who for three months carefully followed their assault on the Babe's home-run record.

"Atta boy 'Jidge,'" Lazzeri shouted to Babe as the Yankees' second baseman made his way to the plate to the cries of "Tony, Tony" from the stadium's Italian denizens who came to watch their boy do good.

Although Little Italy's own came through with a single, Billings settled down and retired the side, forcing Bob Meusel to ground into a double play and Pat Collins to fly out to right. Not that it mattered. A three-run cushion was all Dutch Ruether, the Yankees' veteran lefthander needed to tame the Tigers. Babe loved it. Dutch was his best friend on the club, his roommate on the road, and a man with appetites for liquor and women almost as large as his own.

Ruether greeted the Babe on the infield dirt after he caught Gehringer's pop up to right to end the game. "C'mon keed," the Bambino roared, "I've got a table reserved at the Inn." No matter that Dutch was 33. To Ruth, everyone was "keed."

"Say no more, my large friend," Dutch responded, as his teammates broke out into the familiar chorus of "Roll Out the Barrel" that followed every home victory. "The first round is on me."

◇

THE BLOSSOM HEATH Inn was not the kind of place Morrie ever frequented. In fact it wasn't a place at all; it was an establishment. After Dux games and hurried showers in crowded, dank community center basements, he and his teammates did dance and shmooz with neighborhood friends on the same gym floors on which they played ball. Dinner at Schrafft's, and that only twice, was as fancy as he got. But an establishment that served liquor illegally, featured big bands, dancing, and large crowds of well-dressed people out for a good time—never. Not that his father was against downing a shot of schnapps to celebrate the Sabbath or a birthday, even if it was against the law. There were plenty of ways in Brownsville to get what you wanted—Shikey Friedman and his friends who bootlegged the stuff for Jewish and Italian hoodlums bigger than themselves while offering "protection" to local merchants whether they liked it or not, made sure of that. Dressed in their fancy suits, black-pointed leather Italian shoes, grey fedoras pulled over one eye, covering their slick-backed hair—a caricature each of each other—they all knew Morrie from grade school but had parted ways to pursue a version of the American dream far different from any he fantasized about.

Now here he was, heading towards a place where Shikey would have been right at home, halfway into a September evening, roaring down Merrick Road across the Queens border into the rural climes of Long Island.

"Come on, Ginsberg, I still owe you a dinner from yesterday," Hornsby reminded him as he dressed after the Giants' whitewashed the Pirates for their second victory in a row over the National League's best. "Zack's joining us too."

Morrie agreed to go. Home did not hold much appeal for him. Better to come back to Sackman Street late, when his father was already asleep. Better, maybe, not to go back at all.

Looking out the window, the swirl of woods and flowers passing by, reminded him of summer scenery from the week he and his parents had spent at a bungalow in Loch Sheldrake, New York, the one time there had been money enough for any kind of family vacation. But the Blossom Heath was not Jaffe's Evergreen Manor.

"Are you sure we're still in the United States?" Morrie wondered out loud, as the car turned off onto a gravel circular drive and stopped at their destination—a huge building complete with porticos, columns, vine-covered trellis' lanterns, identified by the imposing front lawn sign as the "Blossom Heath Inn, Harry and Joseph Susskind, proprietors." Only in his world history textbook in Mr. Maloney's class had he seen pictures of any edifice so different, so grand, imposing, and distinct.

The insides of the Blossom Heath Inn were just as exotic. Terrazzo marble floors and wood-paneled foyer walls opened up into a huge ballroom lined in circles with tables full of well-dressed city folk, surrounding an oak dance floor and bandstand that provided opportunity for the evening's entertainment. Sounds of swing emanating outward verified the announcement on the billboard hanging from the front porch that Paul Whiteman and his "Band of Reknown" were already at work.

"Hey, Mr. Weiss, is our table ready?" Zack inquired of a little man with a neatly trimmed goatee, dressed in a black tuxedo, who turned to meet his party of Giants as they stood on the steps leading down to the ballroom floor.

"Certainly Mr. Taylor, we've been expecting you."

"Hey, let me introduce you here to our newest member. You may have read about him in the paper. Morrie Ginsberg meet Mr. David Weiss, the esteemed maître d' of this joint who always takes good care of us."

"Yeah, Davey," Hornsby chuckled, "meet the only half-cocked member of the New York Giants, the 'Rabbi of Swat.'"

"It's a pleasure to meet you Mr. Ginsberg. You are always welcome here."

"Thanks Mr. Weiss, and please just call me Morrie," Morrie replied, shaking hands with his middle-aged host who winked back at him, also ignoring Hornsby's gibe as he escorted his party of three into the ballroom, down front, right of the bandstand, to a large round table with ample room for six.

"Why the big table?" Morrie asked Taylor as they settled into their chairs.

"Didn't Rog tell you? There's some show girls coming over after they're through at Radio City—big baseball fans, if you know what I mean," smiled Morrie's battery mate.

Morrie wasn't quite sure, but he had little time to think about it. His eyes wandered around the room, taking it all in—sights, smells, sounds all new to him—nubile, blond-haired chlorines in low cut silk, bodies bathed in perfume and color beyond the boundaries of his imagination; green salads, red lobsters and white veiny shrimp with their cups of melted butter comfortable on tables laden with plates of roast beef and pork loin—people drinking scotch from tea cups—dancing, chatting, touching, and enjoying—and, except for Mr. Weiss who constantly bustled back and forth welcoming and seating people—not a Jewish face in the crowd, at least not the kind he knew from Sackman Street.

An outburst of loud applause from the tables near the stage momentarily overwhelmed bandstand sounds and drew Morrie's attention to another part of this new world. Turning to see what the commotion was all about, he found the Babe, resplendent in a white linen suit, a beautiful woman on each arm, followed by Ruether, Earl Combs, and several other men and ladies heading across the room to ringside tables reserved for them. Ruth waved to the crowd—confident and comfortable—acknowledging the applause as he walked between tables of well-wishers and backslappers.

"Hello, Babe, good to see you again. Nice going today."

"Thanks Jimmy. Enjoy your dinner," this to New York's own Jimmy Walker, New York's bon vivant mayor and, on any other evening, the Inn's main attraction (Morrie recognized him from the *World*) but tonight just another good friend well-met, no different to the Yankee hero than the well-prepared fan, pen and paper in hand, who stopped him for an autograph—"not for me Babe, but for my kid"—as he continued on to his table.

"A little different from night life in Syracuse?" Hornsby chided, poking Morrie in the ribs as the young pitcher turned back to his teammates while the crowd settled down and resumed its own merriment. Morrie nodded, but before he could fill in the details, waiters and busboys surrounded the table, laying out an array of food as unsettling as everything else he had experienced since they first pulled into the Blossom Heath's driveway.

"Hope you don't mind Morrie but since the meal's on me I took the liberty of ordering for you"—this from the Giants' captain as a waiter placed a large broiled red lobster with claws, tentacles, and eyes in front of him while a busboy tied a huge white bib around his neck.

Not quite the steak and pie á la mode as promised but equally problematic for a Jewish boy from Sackman Street, thought Morrie as he peered down at the traif before him. Although he had played hookey from cheder as much as he went—the dark basement class-room and the old Jewish man with dried food in his beard who smelled as if he never bathed offered less appeal than the fresh air and comraderie of the local schoolyard and streets—Morrie vaguely remembered the admonition in Deuteronomy against eating fish that had no scales. It never made any sense to him; if anything the forbidden offered its own temptation. But this was the first time he ever found himself face to face with a lobster.

Forbidden or not, the prospect was unappealing. While Zack and Hornsby tore into their lobsters with nutcrackers and pointed forks, Morrie blanched at the idea of engaging in similar battle with the tentacled mass in front of him. God's wisdom on the subject of crustaceans suddenly became apparent. Who would want to eat such an ugly, frightening creature that looked like it might eat you first? Better to stick to the salad and rolls. And the "tea," he thought, as he took a sip, no stronger than the brew customary at his own house. Maybe it would settle his stomach. Besides there was too much to see and hear to be bothered with eating.

Especially Ruth and his entourage. Seated at their table across the dance floor from the Giants, the Bambino had occupied center stage since he walked into the inn; waiters, cigarette girls, busboys in constant attendance, elbowing their way to service the Sultan among the inn's patrons who constantly hounded the table. Ruth didn't seem to mind. In fact, as Morrie observed, he obviously enjoyed the attention—shaking hands, signing autographs and laughing heartily at visitors' remarks while gleefully devouring a huge lobster equally as grotesque as the one Morrie chose to ignore.

"What's up Rabbi?" quipped Hornsby, "Isn't the lobster O.K. with you?" First steak and ice cream and now lobster—was the Giants' second sacker a subtle anti-Semite or just a well-meaning team leader ignorant of Jewish tradition, Morrie wondered as he smiled weakly and mumbled something about being too excited to eat— deciding to assume the latter and to avoid a detailed commentary on kashrut and dietary mitzvot.

As if to underline his explanation, Morrie pointed to Paul Whiteman, a large man with gargantuan girth and narrow pencil line moustache, resplendent in his white dinner jacket, black bow tie, a thin baton in his hand, sweat glistening off his round bald head— whose resemblance to Oliver Hardy, at least to Morrie, was striking. Which excited him for even though he knew little about music, he loved the comedy routines of the few Laurel and Hardy kinescopes he had seen, as much for the slapstick as for exotic setting. Lost in the Wild West, afoot in England, aboard ocean liners on the high seas—the boys enticed him to places beyond the familiar, as much reality as metaphor for worlds he wanted to explore.

"Here they go again," mimicked Taylor, "Benny and the Babe on sax for your listening and dancing pleasure." And much to Morrie's surprise, the leader of the "Band of Renown" introduced the two Yankee ballplayers—Benny Bengough, the third string catcher, and baseball's superstar in virtually the same words.

"A weekly ritual," explained Hornsby. "Whiteman always invites them to play along—The Babe just blows a few notes but Benny can really wail."

Morrie's eyes remained fixed on Ruth as he and Bengough made their way to the bandstand to the applause of the crowd. Just like those Blossom Heath patrons who had rushed the Babe's table to be in his presence, Morrie intently followed his every move on the bandstand—watching Ruth joke with the musicians, pretend to warm up, and finally settle in to play with the band. So much so that he did not notice the arrival of the three show girls at his table that Hornsby had arranged for or the note he slipped to Davey Weiss, with whispered instructions to take it up to Whiteman. Only a firm nudge on the shoulder by the Giant captain brought him out of his gaze and face to face with yet another test of who he was.

"Morrie, this is Doris, Jeanette, and Yvonne." "Girls, this is Morrie Ginsberg, the famous Rabbi of Swat," chuckled Hornsby as he motioned them to sit down, Jeanette next to Taylor, Yvonne almost in his own lap, and Doris next to the thoroughly embarrassed and flushed Giant rookie.

Dry-tongued, lock-jawed, unnerved by the introduction, Morrie said nothing, taking in women he only dreamed about. Mama, bubbe, neighborhood girls—zaftig, big-boned, dark-haired, dressed in cotton, cleanly-scrubbed, greasy-skinned no make-up faces, makers of homes or workers in sweatshops, keepers of tradition, thoroughly familiar and Jewish—these were the women in his life. Jeannette, Yvonne, and Doris were not; thin and blond, shimmering in spangles and silk, powdered, rouged, and perfumed, show girls and fantasy makers still exuberant from their night on the boards at Radio City and ready for a good time.

Not that Morrie made all those connections at once or that the trio were any more identical triplets than the women of Sackman Street. In fact, at the moment, all he could think of was first, lobsters, now shicksas. . . . Gevalt, what a curious night this was turning out to be—his body literally aquiver as he forced a smile while Mr. Weiss held out a chair for Doris as she slithered in next to him.

While Yvonne and Jeannette warmly renewed their acquaintances with their Giant regulars—"What's a rabbi, honey?" Yvonne cooed into Hornsby's ear as he poured her some "tea"—Morrie took in more of Doris—too shy and inexperienced to know what to say or do but attracted by her beauty.

Never before had he been so close to so different a woman. Puberty had come and gone, yet Morrie remained virtually uninvolved with any girls—except in his fantasies and occasional wet, sticky sheets—let alone someone who looked like Doris. As a little boy he was aware of the sounds of bedsprings and the muffled voices emanating several times a week from his parents' bedroom soon after they went to bed, followed by his father's footsteps on the way to the bathroom and the inevitable flush of the toilet, which, as he found from his own nocturnal trips to the same place, did not always wash away curious clear, oval shaped bags that appeared in the bowl on those nights when his father preceded him. A sad, empty feeling mixed with relief always followed—Morrie's recognition that no matter how often he might win the battle with Jake for Mama's affections, certain prizes were not for him. As he grew older and learned about condoms—"scumbags" among his friends—he occasionally "borrowed" a Trojan from his father's night table drawer and slipped it on in the privacy of his own bed, reveling in a fantasy world of Harlows and Bows and even once his cousin Sarah from the Bronx—always making sure that when he finished, unlike his father, the toilet did its job.

But this was no fantasy. Here he was, sitting next to a woman who was there for the express purpose of enjoying herself. Not at a wedding, bar mitzvah or Passover seder crowded into a basement social hall or the confining narrowness of brownstone flats, but in a nightclub on a warm September evening rich with unfamiliar sounds, smells, and sights as intoxicating as the exotic prospect of Doris, who, as even Morrie noticed, was growing increasingly irritated by his enraptured silence.

"So you dance for a living?"

Dance for a living! Women he knew his mother's age stayed home and did what they were supposed to do; preparing their daughters to do the same, even those who did take the train to work every day in a Manhattan shirt factory. But dancing? Living outside the family? Not on Sackman Street. Maybe, "once in a blue moon," as his mother would say—taken by the phrase that somehow made her feel more American than she felt in her heart. . . .

"Six nights a week with matinees Wednesday and Saturday,"

Doris shot back, regretting at once her sharp tone and Morrie's reddened face, suddenly aware of how painfully shy her companion for the evening really was.

"And you play baseball for the Giants—I guess we're both in the entertainment business," she laughed softly, hoping that she hadn't offended Morrie, this man so different looking from her usual dates, whom she found curiously attractive.

"Well, I just came up to New York. . . ."

"Why so modest, boy?" interrupted Hornsby, as Morrie began to explain. "C'mon Doris, don't you read the papers—this here is that Jew boy, the famous Rabbi of Swat—the greatest thing since sliced bread whose gonna lead us to the Promised Land and make McGraw rich."

"Take it easy Captain," Taylor broke in. "A little less scotch and a little more care with your mouth—no need to rag Morrie. He's an alright kid."

Feelings gripped Morrie's body that he had experienced once before but dreamed about more times than he could remember—dreams replaying reality. Wandering down the wrong block on the way home from school by himself when he was ten. Surrounded by five Irish kids a few years older than himself. Cries of Christ Killer, Kike, Jew Bastard. Rage and anger building within; rising up and beating the crap out of his assailants. That was the dream. Reality was a bit different. Five toughs knocked him down, one held his arms to the pavement, another his legs. The others unzipped his pants, pulled out his cock and urinated on him—warm Irish piss on cold skin and concrete.

"Look, Eddie, the fucking kike's steaming," one shouted, as Morrie writhed in humiliation. Eventually they let him up. He ran home, never telling his parents what had happened and terrified for days after whenever he went outside.

Pissed on again? Caught between the boy of his youth and the man of his dreams? Or was Hornsby just ragging him like Zack said? After all he had invited him to dinner. And he hadn't given him a second look since he shot his mouth off; his attention focused on the bandstand where Benny and the Babe continued to wail.

Unsure of what to do, Morrie said nothing. Instinctively, Doris reached over and nestled his right hand in hers; a sympathetic gesture that startled him even more. Tormented and tempted by everything the night offered, Morrie maintained his silence and smiled in return. Leaving his hand enclosed in hers; comforted by the soft skinned, red-nailed fingers entwined around his own, all he could think of at that moment was that he was thankful he was not Burtie Finkelstein: fellow Dux and school boy friend whose ever sweaty palms ("Nothing to worry about Mrs. Finkelstein," the doctor told his mother when she asked about her son's condition, "it's just a phase he is passing through") provoked laughter among his friends and terror too, for fear that he might touch them with his slimy hands.

"What are you smiling about Morrie?" Doris asked, returning the expression in kind.

"Oh, it's nothing. I was just thinking of an old friend of mine, that's all."

"What about him?"

"Nothing. Really, nothing. . . ."

"Hey Morrie, pipe down will you. I want to hear what's happening up there," this from Hornsby, himself all smiles, as he gestured to the bandstand.

Suddenly aware that the raucous sounds of the Blossom Inn's patrons and the music they came to listen to had stopped, Morrie turned too—everyone attentive to Paul Whiteman as he asked for quiet and motioned the Babe to the microphone while holding a scrap of paper in his hand.

"Babe, I've got a message here from your old friend Rogers Hornsby who tells me that there's someone in the audience that you and all the folks should meet. He's a new boy in town, here tonight with his friends and teammates from the New York Giants. I hear that he is anxious to say hello to you. O.K. folks, let's give a big Blossom Heath Inn welcome to the Giants' new pitcher, Muggsy McGraw's answer to the Sultan of Swat—Morrie Ginsberg, the Rabbi of Swat! Come on up Morrie and take a bow."

The Babe laughed, Morrie trembled, and the rhythmic clapping of men and women eager for their own enjoyment filled the room.

"He's right over here Whitey," Hornsby shouted over the din. Standing up on his chair, arms waving wildly above his head, the Giants' captain orchestrated the moment until the incessant glare of spotlights in search of their victim fell on Morrie and Doris.

Friends! Had his father been right about McConnell's column? Is this the kind of attention he wanted? Turning away from the lights, Morrie caught a glimpse of Ruth joking with his saxophone-playing sidekick while Whiteman beckoned him to the stage.

". . . There was ease in Specs Hills' manner and a smile on Traynor's face / For they figured they had Morrie in the tightest sort of place. . . ."

"I'll count to five. If you're not here by then, why then we'll just come down and get you ourselves, right Babe?"

Ruth just shrugged his shoulders and took a step away from the bandleader.

"One . . . Two. . . ." With each shouted number a growing chorus of voices joined Whiteman, urging Morrie on.

"You better go up there," Taylor encouraged, "or they'll never let you off the hook. Just say hello, shake hands with Ruth and come back."

Morrie nodded, pulled away from Doris, pushed his chair away from the table, and made his way to the stage to meet his "namesake."

"That's a boy, Morrie," Whiteman greeted him. "Shake hands here with the Sultan of Swat."

Morrie extended his hand to the Babe who immediately engulfed it in his huge mitts. "Nice to meet you keed, Good luck with the Giants. Maybe we'll see you in the Series."

"Thanks, Mr. Ruth," Morrie stammered, attempting a quick exit from the stage.

"Not so fast, boy," Whiteman bellowed as he grabbed him by the arm. "It's not very often that my stage is graced by a sultan and a rabbi at the same time. Tell everybody how you got your name."

"Forget it Paul," the Babe bellowed, "Folks here want to dance and listen to me play the horn, right keed? See you around. Now get outta here and enjoy yourself."

With that, the Babe winked at Morrie, turned around to the orchestra and began to play. Whiteman let go of Morrie's arm and waved his baton in beat with the band. The Pride of Sackman Street took his cue, fled the bandstand and ran out into the night.

◇

MERRICK ROAD LOOKED a good deal less inviting than it had a few hours earlier, summer pastoral replaced by more ominous shades of nighttime darkness more in keeping with Morrie's mood. The panic and anxiety that gripped him when Whiteman called out his name—his body shaking, the tightness around his heart, soaked in sweat from head to toe—had subsided, leaving him cold in the cool September night. Enraged by Hornsby's attacks but unable to retort, enticed by Doris's difference but too overwhelmed to respond, the butt of Whiteman's good-natured play but too mortified to participate, thankful for Ruth's good humor but unable to enjoy it—all in all a less than impressive evening for the Rabbi of Swat.

The sound of tires crunching on loose shoulder gravel jostled Morrie out of his thoughts.

"Are you planning to make it to the Polo Grounds by tomorrow, or would you like a ride into the city?" Doris inquired, shouting over the noise of the idling engine of her roadster that had pulled along-side him.

"So, you drive too? I should have known," Morrie said as he opened the car door and sat down next to her. "What about your friends? Are they planning to dance their way to Radio City?"

Doris said nothing, pulled her car back on the road and headed towards the city.

Not that Morrie gave her a chance to respond. "I'm sorry, really I am. Thanks for the lift. I really hadn't thought how I would get back."

"Forget it. Rog and Zack will take care of the girls. And don't apologize to me. You've had a rough night—everyone's entitled."

Morrie took his eyes off the road in front of him and glanced over at Doris as she talked. Intent on her driving, hands clasped firmly and confidently around the leather steering wheel, her face profiled in the shadowy cast of moonlight that came in through the windshield, she was like no other woman he had ever known. And yet, removed from the noise and excitement of the Blossom Heath, he felt strangely comfortable and excited by her side.

"I looked pretty stupid in there, didn't I?"

"Stupid? I wouldn't call it stupid. Frightened, maybe . . . intimi-dated . . . a bit overwhelmed, but not stupid."

"That sounds a little better."

"Better than what?"

"Stupid! That's what my father would say about tonight. Stupid for sticking your head in places where you don't belong."

"The Blossom Heath?"

"Paul Whiteman never played Loew's Pitkin!"

"I don't think I understand."

Morrie chuckled. "You're looking at a man who for the first time in his life stared a lobster in the face, went to dinner in the same place with the mayor of New York, met Babe Ruth and survived. And all in your company—a woman who dances for a living, drives cars and picks up strangers wandering aimlessly on Long Island in the middle of the night. You're not from here, are you?"

"You mean New York?"

"Of course, what else would I mean?"

"I don't know. The way you were going on, maybe you thought I came from across the ocean from some foreign land."

"No. That's where I come from."

"I still don't understand. . . ."

"I know. Let's just say. . . ."

"And what is all this about the Rabbi of Swat? I never met a rabbi but I didn't think they looked like you."

"You don't read the sportspages, do you? Don't you know that you are sitting next to the Rabbi of Swat?"

"That much I know. Tell me more."

"About a week ago, the Giants called me up from Syracuse. The papers made a big deal about how this hometown Jewish boy would help the Giants at the gate. Some sportswriter nicknamed me the Rabbi of Swat; you know, a play on what they call the Babe. Two days ago I got a start against the Pirates. To make a long story short, I pitched a good game, got the winning hit, and packed the stands with Jewish people who thrilled to see one of their own make good."

"And tonight you shared the spotlight with Babe. A show girl's fantasy!" Doris laughed.

"I don't see what's so funny."

"Oh, I'm sorry. I wasn't laughing at you. It's just that your predicament is a Rockette's dream. Chorus line to top billing! A star is born! Another Ruth, no less?"

"That remains to be seen."

"I thought so," Doris chuckled. "I could see how much fun you were having in there."

Now it was Morrie's turn to laugh. Uncontrollably, loudly, into the night, out the car window, down Merrick Road, from the Blossom Heath to Brownsville, across the Harlem River from the Polo Grounds to Yankee Stadium, rumbling through Wall Street caverns, up Broadway from the Village to Washington Heights, lustfully filling the city with his desires.

"I didn't know I was such a comedian."

"I'm sorry, really I am," Morrie gasped, finally catching his breath. "It's just that you . . . Where did you say you were from?"

"You really have to stop doing that."

"Doing what?"

"Apologizing for every other word you say."

"I'm sorry. . . ." And now they both laughed—together—until Morrie broke in. "It's an old habit. I'll do my best. But you didn't answer my question."

"What question?"

"Where are you from?"

"A small town in Michigan, Grand Rapids."

"Grand Rapids, Michigan. Population 158,000, 66 miles west of the state capital, Lansing. The furniture capital of the Middle West, home of Baker furniture, heavily Dutch. . . ."

It was all Doris could do to keep her eyes on the road, so startled was she by Morrie's encyclopedic rendition of her home town. "How do you know all that?" she exclaimed.

"It's in the Almanac."

"In the Almanac? You mean to tell me that you memorized the Almanac?"

Morrie smiled. "Only the parts I'm interested in. American geography—cities—to be specific. In fact, any place with a population over 20,000 outside of a fifty mile radius of New York is fair game, meticuously put to memory, state by state, during study hall at Boys High, starting with Alabama, which took almost no time, there being few places beyond Birmingham and Tuscaloosa to keep track of, Tuscaloosa, for example, 60 miles southwest of the state capital, Birmingham. Home of the Tuscaloosa Giants, population 65,000, heavily curious about a Jewish boy playing America's Game in their backyard—something he learned first-hand and from headlines in the local rag, 'See the Jew Boy at Second Today,' all the way to Wyoming."

Doris chuckled. "Oh, I see."

"You do?" Morrie responded, surprised.

"Sure, you never know when it might come in handy. On your travels, I mean."

"We can only hope."

———

[Three peas in a pod, Dorie, Morrie and Me. Grand Rapids, Baltimore, Brownsville—it doesn't really matter. Not back then or maybe ever. True, we don't know much about Doris's background yet, but the key is less the fathers than the sons, or daughters, in her case. All this angst about fathers not loving their children enough, not telling them, hugging them, smiling at them enough . . . Enough already! It's not the whole story. Never was, never will be. Shit, the world was out there for us to explore, to taste, to be in it and of it. Read Fitzgerald, for God's sake! He's right on the mark. And while we're at it, what's this stuff about my winking good humor? It was bad enough having to share the stage with old Benny! Besides the kid was dripping so badly that if he stayed up there any longer we all would have been swimming!]

―――――――――

―――

"Speaking of geography, where would you like me to drop you off?"

"I don't know. Do you mind if we just drive a while more?"

Doris smiled, reached over and squeezed Morrie's hand. This time he didn't flinch.

◇

WASHINGTON WAS NOT Babe's favorite town. Not that the Senators posed a problem. By September 14th, when the Yankees moved into Griffith Park to open a four game set, the nation's baseball club was buried in fourth, twenty-one games behind the Yankees. Even Walter "Big Train" Johnson posed little threat in the waning moments of his great career. And even with Prohibition, the nation's capital still provided ample place for Babe's post game enjoyments.

The plain truth was that D.C. was just too close to Baltimore. Too close to his father's dock-side saloon on West Camden Street, its dark interiors permanently scarred by the smells of stale beer and tobacco. Too close to memories of his poor mother, always tired and sad, and his years at St. Mary's. . . .

"It's only for a little while Georgie," his father told him, when he turned the nine-year-old over to the Xaverian Brothers for the first time in 1904.

"With your mother sick, the tavern to run, all your brothers and sisters to watch out for and you always getting into trouble stealing and fighting, I just need to have them look after you for a while."

And so it was; the first time. The boy said nothing when he left or returned. No protest nor promise to behave. At twelve, after his mother died, Little George, as he was called to distinguish him from his father whose name he carried, was back at St. Mary's for good— the place where he discovered baseball, where boys younger than himself looked up to him as their hero, where Xaverian brothers encouraged him to be a man and where he learned to be one, fighting his own battles until there was no one bigger than himself to fight. It wasn't Babe then, just Georgie, "Nig," or "Niggerlips. . . ."

———

[Now hold on a minute! I told you before, everyone knows all about my childhood. There's no need to keep bringing it up. Besides life at St. Mary's was not all so bad. I learned a lot there. Shit, I can still iron my own shirts, not that I have to any more. Do you think you'd be writing about me now if I stayed at home? Believe me, there wasn't much time for baseball on West Camden. Do you think Jack Dunn would have found me there? Jack Dunn? You know, the owner of the Baltimore Orioles, my first professional team? And I did get home about once a month, at least until my mother died. After that, well . . . I do remember one Christmas. . . .]

———

"Come on 'Niggerlips,' let's see how tough you are. . . ."

"Hey Babe, pay attention up there before Ciddy strikes you out," Miller Huggins jokingly called out as Ruth, preoccupied by taunting schoolyard memories, swung half-heartedly at a grapefruit delivered by Ciddy Durst, the Yankees' utility outfielder and batting practice pitcher.

Leaning against the batting cage, Tris Speaker, the Senators' center fielder, joined in. "What's the matter Jidge, hitting like that kept you a pitcher in Boston. Too much of the good life last night?"

"In Washington?" Babe retorted, joining Speaker behind the cage. The two had known each other since 1914 when Ruth came to the Red Sox as a pitcher and Speaker dominated the outfield for Boston. In 1915, the lanky Texan known as "Spoke" batted .322 and led the Red Sox to the pennant and a World Series drubbing of Philadelphia. The Babe chipped in with eighteen victories and even managed twenty-nine hits. Friends ever since, their paths rarely crossed outside the diamond.

"Everything set for tomorrow?"

"Yes. I got us a ten o'clock tee off time at National. You think you'll be out of bed by then?"

"I'll be there with bells on," Babe laughed.

"Good. And bring plenty of cash. My game's improved since we last met."

——————
——

True to his word, Speaker pulled up in front of the Shoreham a few minutes after nine, his thirty-nine-year-old frame almost recovered from the drubbing administered by the Yankees the day before. Glad for the day off, he was almost as happy when Babe backed out of their golf date at the end of the game and asked him to come by anyway for a day's excursion to Baltimore.

"What's your pleasure?" Speaker asked, as Ruth lumbered out the hotel's doors and entered Tris's Ford sedan.

"Let's just head down and play it by ear, if that's O.K. with you."

"No problem. I've got no major plans, Speaker replied," as he pulled away from the curb and blended in with the morning traffic down Constitution Avenue.

"Did you see the paper this morning? It looks like the Giants are making a good run at it. You may not be doing much traveling come World Series time."

Babe smiled. "To tell you the truth, Spoke, I didn't get by the descriptions of the two home runs I hit yesterday to squash you guys. Who'd they play?"

"They shut out St. Louis—swept the series, and are now only 1 and $1/2$ back of the Pirates. Some rookie pitcher named Ginsberg did the job. Even hit a home run to boot."

"I ran into the kid a few weeks ago in New York. He beat the Pirates in his first start and the papers made a big deal about it—called him the Rabbi of Swat or something like that. Wrote a poem about him and his Jew fans."

"Yeah. The paper mentioned something about half of Brooklyn travelling to the Bronx to see their boy make good. How did you meet him?"

"At the Blossom Heath. Benny and me were doing our usual bit with the band when Whiteman calls up this kid. It was right after his first win. You should have seen him. They turned the spot on him at his table. He looked scared shitless, frozen to his chair. I could see that fucker Hornsby laughing his head off and figured the bastard was up to his usual. Anyway, finally this kid. . . . what's his name, Greenberg?"

"Ginsberg."

"Yeah, Ginsberg. Anyway, finally he gets up and makes it to the stage. I mean, I thought he was going to shit in his pants. He looked so bad and nervous. I shook hands with the kid. Shit, it was like taking a bath."

"What do you mean?"

"I mean his hands were soaked with sweat."

" I bet he throws a mean spitter."

"Yeah," Babe chuckled. "Anyway, then Paul tries to make him stay up there and tell everyone how come he's called the Rabbi of Swat. The poor kid didn't know what to do, so I stepped in; said something about wanting to play or something like that, and got him off the hook. He took off like a bat out of hell."

Speaker smiled. "You're a piece of work Babe."

"What'd you mean?"

"Helping him out like that."

Babe smiled, nestled back in the Ford's lush leather seat, content to let the warm September sun play on his broad face. "It was no big deal. Hey, I'll tell you what Spoke. How about we get some soft shelled crabs down by the docks. I'll even give you a tour of my old neighborhood, but first a chance to save your soul at St. Mary's."

"At your service Oh Sultan," Speaker replied, as he deftly moved the sedan through traffic and onto the ramp leading to the main road between Washington and Baltimore. But remember. I'm an Episcopalian."

Not that it mattered. An hour later, off the highway now, southwest of downtown but well within city limits, Speaker, directed by

Ruth, street map in lap, perplexed by unfamiliar streets and land-
marks that were not part of his memory, pointed the Ford up one
block and down another, in search of his youth.

"Are you sure it's on Wilkins' Avenue?"

"Yeah, I'm sure," Babe answered, tossing the map into the
backseat. "Just head up the hill. I don't recognize anything around
here but I know we were up on the hill. And that smell, that hasn't
changed."

"What is that shit? It smells like Chicago."

"Our very own stock yards, Baltimore's answer to Chicago's
finest, about a half mile past St. Mary's. We used to pray for wind-
shifts. Look, there it is," Babe exclaimed, pointing ahead to a chain-
linked fence, grey rusting metal ten feet high extending a whole city
block, containing within a large main brick building, three stories
high, surrounded by several smaller, wooden structures radiating
out like struts from it towards the road.

But it wasn't St Mary's. Not any longer. This they learned from
the guard at the gate of Red Star Meat Packing Plant #2, a burly-faced
German fellow who informed them that the Catholic Diocese had
sold the grounds five years ago, the main building long since gutted
of orphans and Brothers along with its classrooms, dining hall, gym-
nasium, and offices to make room for casings, cooking vats, and con-
veyor belts; the three dormitories converted to final packing areas
for the array of salami and sausage featuring the Red Star label.

"Where to now, Babe?" Speaker asked. "You ready for some
crabs?"

"Yeah, sure. Just head down to the docks. I know a place on
Front Street that will take good care of us, if it's still there. Shit, I
really wanted you to meet Brother Matthias."

"Forget it. What about the old neighborhood you were going to show me?"

"After lunch, Tris, we'll see."

Two hours later, stuffed with beer, clam chowder and crabcakes, topped off by a wedge of lemon meringue pie at a place that was still there—The Sea Shanty—a hole in the wall wooden-planked, five table room open for breakfast and lunch only catering to fishermen and dockworkers and local denizens like George Ruth Sr. who every once in a while sent his boy down to pick up a few crabcakes for dinner. . . .

———————
———

[I loved that place. Once a week, when I was five, every Friday around three o'clock, my father would give me fifty cents and send me off to Manny's. That's what we called it. "Tell Manny it's for me and make sure they're fresh," he shouted, as I ran down the street, every Friday the same. And Manny always expecting me. "Ten crabcakes like usual, right Georgie?" he always asked even though he knew the answer, pinching my cheek and patting my face as he took my money and sat me down while he went back into the kitchen to get the cakes, each wrapped in paper, crispy-greased hot, that soaked through the brown paper bag by the time I made it the five blocks back to our house above the bar, time enough to suck out the crab meat in the small claws that Manny always gave me—"our little secret," he said. And then my mother would take the cakes and put them in the oven for dinner, one for each of us and two for my father who never had time to sit down when we ate, always busy on Fridays especially with fishermen and dockworkers, beaten by their

— 65 —

week's work but bouyed by the jingle of their labor and the prospect of a few hard shots and chasers before they went home.]

––––––––––––––––

––––

"Good to see you again, Babe. How long has it been since you were down here?" Shanty owner Herman Manheim inquired as the ballplayer prepared to leave.

"It's been a while Manny," Babe responded. "At least a few years, that's for sure."

"Showing Mr. Speaker around your old haunts?"

"That's the general idea."

"Well, say hello to your father when you see him. He hasn't been in for a while."

"Sure, Manny, I will."

But he didn't. Oh, they went by the bar on West Camden where George Senior still lived above his business, now alone, a widower, all his children either dead or scattered except for one daughter who lived on the other side of the city and whom he visited every other Sunday for dinner. Babe pointed it out to Speaker as they drove slowly by without stopping, past the house on Frederick Street where he remembered living for a year or so when his family moved in with his grandparents on his mother's side and then down Emery Street to 216 which he didn't remember but knew was the house in which he had been born.

"Are you sure you don't want to say hello to your father?" Speaker asked as they drove by the bar.

"No, that's alright kid," Babe responded, solemnly staring out the car's side window. "I'll catch him some other time. We've got to be heading back."

"Whatever you say Babe, whatever you say."

8

MORRIE'S ROAD TRIP had its own rhythm, punctuated by railroad porters and engineers who transported the Giants to Chicago, then Philadelphia and on to Pittsburgh in quest of the National League flag. Although his teammates found nothing novel or exhilarating about a season's travel grinding to an end, he marveled at it all. Although trying to hang on, let alone sleep, in Pullman upperberth hammocks presented a formidable and uncomfortable challenge, breakfast served by Negro men dressed in white starched shirts and black trousers at dining car tables set for royalty—or so Morrie imagined—each with their own white, starched tablecloth covered with real silver and white china, more than compensated for the lack of a full night's sleep. Never a big eater, especially in the morning when a hunk of pumpernickel and a glass of milk usually sufficed, setting and place provided its own sustenance.

So too did the sounds and sights at every stop. The bleating of thousands of cattle mixed with the acrid smell of their own waste and death as the American Limited chugged by Chicago's stock-yards on its way into the palatial vastness of Union Station. The splendor of the Palmer House where McGraw put the Giants up, only three short blocks from Spalding's Sporting Goods Emporium on Madison Street—two stories of bats, balls, gloves, clothing, bicycles, tennis racquets, golf clubs, fishing rods, exercise machines, and assorted sporting paraphernalia as exotic to Morrie as the Victorian excesses of Marshall Field's where Zack took him to help pick out a present for Doris, who he had not stopped thinking about since that night she picked him up on Merrick Road. The simplicity and stateliness of Independence Hall that captured the nation's beginnings. Even the grimy, coal-laden faces of Pittsburgh steel-workers emerging from a day's labor amidst the clang and heat of their mills—each held their own attraction for this young man, always taken with the excitement of new places since he first traveled away from Brownsville with the Dux in search of basketball conquests.

And the people in each city, at least the Jewish ones, found their own attraction in him. Even as the Limited pulled out of Grand Central, McGraw took Morrie aside in the smoking lounge and gave him his road game marching orders, all the while puffing on a hand-rolled Cuban cigar, far more aromatic and mild than the Bering Plazas of a Brownsville childhood.

"Look, Morrie, I hear that there are some kind of ceremonies planned in each park when you pitch—local clubs, organizations—you know, of people who admire you. Some may even invite you out to dinner or ask you to speak at a meeting. Do your best to go along with it. It's good for you and for business as long as it doesn't interfere with your pitching."

Mesmerized by the sweet smell of tobacco and the lateness of the hour, his head more fixed on what a Cuban cigar might taste like and if McGraw would offer him one (once, when he was nine, after supper, he persuaded his father to let him take a puff of his precious Plaza. One deep draw on top of roast chicken and potato latkes and Morrie threw up all over the kitchen table, disgusting Jake and humiliating himself), Morrie nodded in agreement, not at all clear exactly what McGraw had in mind but too tired to worry about it. Two days later, warming up behind first base at Wrigley Field, he received his first taste of what his skipper meant.

"Gevalt, it looks like Morrie Ginsberg Day," laughed Zack, pointing behind Morrie as he tossed the ball back to his pitcher.

Morrie turned around. No more than thirty feet from him, coming out of their seats along the left-field line, walking towards home plate, came a band of some thirty men who Morrie knew were Jewish. Not that they tried to hide it. Some carried banners with Morrie's name on them as well as the organizations they represented—"B'nai B'rith Welcomes Morrie to Chicago," "The Free Sons of Israel, Lodge Number Nine's Favorite Son," "The Amalgamated Cutters of Chicago Love Morrie." Others had their hands full with packages while the rest simply waved to the crowd as the Cubs' announcer, megaphone in hand, informed the crowd that it was time to honor the Giants' visiting pitcher, Morrie Ginsberg, "The Rabbi of Swat."

"I don't believe this," Morrie shouted to Zack, who just stood there and smiled above the growing applause and noise that greeted the entourage as it made its way down the line. Before Morrie had a chance to deliver another pitch, Joe McCarthy, Chicago's manager, along with McGraw, walked over to him, each taking him by an arm, and escorted him to home plate—an honor guard of Irish Catholics for the young Jewish hero.

Shaking hands all around, Morrie smiled nervously and muttered his thanks as representatives of each group presented him with their gifts—freshly-baked challah still warm in its brown paper wrapper, a new suit of clothes from the Amalgamated gang, and even a state of the art "Spalding" fishing jacket, full of extra pockets and slits to hold the angler's each and every lure.

"Strange Jews, these Midwesterners," he thought, as he slipped the jacket over his uniform and posed for a photographer with Phil Agronsky, the president of the Free Sons of Israel. This from a young man whose most meaningful experience with fish remained limited to sitting on the toilet in his bathroom at Sackman Street when he was ten, feeding rye bread to a large carp languishing in the bathtub. "Abie," he called him, the only "pet" he ever had, who gasped for air for three days before being sacrificed for his mother's Passover gefilte fish.

"Not so fast, boychik," Agronsky whispered into Morrie's ear as the Giant pitcher tried to head back to the dugout. Grabbing him by the arm, he pulled Morrie back to homeplate. "I got a short speech all prepared and then maybe we could hear from you. Nu?"

Shades of the Blossom Heath all over again, thought the Giants' new gate attraction as he waited for this new master of ceremonies to begin.

Morrie needn't have worried. Phil wasted no words. A tailor by trade but known among his friends for his oratorical skills honed in union halls and lodge meetings, he proceeded to recount Morrie's glorious debut against the Pirates and read "Ginsberg at the Bat," much to the delight of the spectators sitting around home plate who could make out his words, even adding his own verse, written especially for the occasion:

"There is music in the ghetto as the daylight peters out;
There is many a wild falsetto as the children laugh and shout,
And the saxophones are blowin', and the citizens are crowin'
As they think of Morrie Ginsberg and his famous two-base clout."

"Thanks for letting us celebrate with you," Agronsky concluded, shaking the young pitcher's hand, which was surprisingly dry, given the occasion. "And don't be too hard on us Cubs."

Instead of running off center stage, this time Morrie managed to wave to the stands and say "thank you." He then proceeded to whitewash the hometown nine, already mired in fifth place, allowing only scratch singles to Jolly Cholly Grimm and to Gabby Hartnett.

It was the same in Philadelphia. Well, almost the same. Again, Jewish organizations had their "day" with Morrie. It did get a little awkward when the local faithful presented him with a warm pot of chicken soup and kreplach and a two-foot-long kisha for the train ride to Pittsburgh. After handing the worst club in the National League a 6–2 defeat—the Giants' fifth victory in a row that pulled them to within one game of the Pirates—Morrie and his teammates retired to their locker room for a quick shower and snack before heading to the station.

"What is that shit?" Hornsby groused to no one in particular as he walked past a clubhouse table laden with the usual assortment of sausage, cold-cuts, potato salad and bread as well as Morrie's gifts.

"C'mon Rog," Zack answered, his mouth full of a large piece of derma, casing and all, "When was the last time you saw cow gut served up so well?"

Mel Ott and Bill Terry did a double-take that would have done Eddie Cantor proud, simultaneously spitting out of their mouths what had been, up to then, a new and delicious taste for them. No words from Taylor, who proceeded to explain the composition of this Jewish delicacy, could persuade them to try again.

Pittsburgh, too, had its own twist. Scheduled to pitch the last game of the three-game set against right hander Ray Kremer, Morrie looked forward to an evening out on the town with Ott and Taylor, his closest companions on the road. But an hour after the club checked into the Park Sheraton, persistent knocking on Morrie's hotel room door summoned him from his shower to the lobby. "Mr. McGraw wants to see you right away," the bell hop informed him. "He says to make sure you look respectable."

Five minutes later, his bristly black hair still damp, Morrie descended the Sheraton's grand staircase to encounter not only McGraw but another man, who heartily grabbed his hand even before they had been introduced.

"So John, dis is the boy who is making so much noise, and such a little vonce too."

Morrie smiled nervously, trying to place the neatly dressed man before him—shorter even than McGraw with oversized ears and a nose that marked him as a landsman but who spoke a mixture of English and German with a decidedly southern accent that reminded him of Zack. Maybe, he mused, this was some long-lost relative of his catcher friend, whose knowledge of Jewish idiom and food continued to surprise him.

"Morrie, let me introduce you to Barney Dreyfuss, the Pirates' owner. Mr. Dreyfuss, here, would like you to meet some of his friends for dinner tonight. Since you're not pitching until Thursday and you have to eat anyway, I told him that would be fine. Whaddya say Ginsberg?"

"Well, sir, I had sort of made plans to go out with some of the boys. If it's alright with Mr. Dreyfuss, could we do it. . . ."

"Tomorrow is no good Johnny. We have something special planned for tonight," Dreyfuss interjected.

"You heard Mr. Dreyfuss, boy. How about it?"

"Sure," Morrie replied, not that he could say no even if he wanted to. But the truth was the invitation was exciting, even if he had no choice. It wasn't every day that the owner of the Pittsburgh Pirates demanded his presence at dinner, a man, he remembered, as he stood there listening to others decide his evening, whose picture he had once seen in the *Forward* alongside a column, not in Yiddish, which he couldn't read, but on the Sunday English page, that praised him as an American success.

Expecting an intimate little dinner with Dreyfuss and a few of his friends—"probably some rabbi will offer his daughter to you under the chupah," Taylor chided Morrie as he put on his best suit, indeed his only suit in preparation for the evening—the Giants' own Jewish leader found himself instead center stage on a dais before some 100 of Pittsburgh's finest Jewish citizens, gathered together for the annual awards meeting of the Squirrel Hill B'nai B'rith, presided over by none other than the diminutive president of the Pittsburgh Pirates.

As it turned out, Zack wasn't far off in his predictions. Although no offers for immediate matrimony were forthcoming, one Samuel Cohen, president of the Irene Kaufman Settlement House, who sat next to him, assured Morrie that he had a beautiful daughter he would love for him to take out on the town, at his expense, of course, and with his blessing. Morrie listened politely to the pitch, dutifully accepted the scrap of paper offered him with name and address, begged off because of his upcoming start, and promised to get in touch next year if he was still with the Giants when they came back to Pittsburgh.

Although disappointed that he could not persuade Morrie to take him up on his offer, Mr. Cohen cheered as loudly as anyone when Dreyfuss introduced the Giant rookie to his audience as "the greatest Jewish baseball player since Lip Pike, a true son of Israel and America" who, in his own way, was making his "own contributions that all Jews could be proud of." Aware of his own stake in the Giants-Pirates series, the Pirates' owner did ask that Morrie not do too much damage to the Pirates' pennant hopes when he pitched on Thursday.

"May you pitch well for seven innings, be relieved with the score tied, and then watch us win in the ninth," Dreyfuss declared, sitting down as he directed Morrie to the podium.

Morrie struggled to his feet, consumed as much by the emotion of the evening as by the chicken soup, gefilte fish, and roast chicken he had eaten.

"Much more I cannot expect from my closest enemies," he replied, a spontaneous response escaping his lips before he had a chance to think about his own timidity in the face of friendly strangers, who, much to his surprise, laughed warmly at his retort.

"I just want to thank Mr. Dreyfuss for inviting me tonight and for this wonderful dinner. To tell you the truth, although I like hotel food, I don't think they serve gefilte fish at the Park Sheraton," Morrie continued, on a roll now, outside himself, observing his enjoyment of the evening, the steady appreciation of his audience, his growing ease with the moment.

"It's an honor to be here and to be honored by you. And although I am a little early, I wish you all a Happy New Year." With that Morrie smiled and sat down to the loud applause of his dinner companions.

———————————

———

"If only Jake could have been here tonight," he wondered, as he drove back to his hotel in Dreyfuss's chauffeured limousine. "Maybe he could begin to see that what I do is no disgrace. I wonder what he would make of Zack. Maybe I should invite him to Rosh Hashanah," he laughed to himself, wondering at the same time whether he was still welcome in his father's home or whether he really cared. Truly a confusing time, rich with a variety of experience, loaded with pleasure and pain—ripe stuff for a young man familiar with the complexities of the Talmud who chose to play baseball for a living in a country that honored its athletic heroes as if they were Moses or Rabbi Akiba.

◇

MAMA HAD SIMILAR thoughts as she sat at the kitchen table. Not about ancient Jewish heroes but about her boy and his father.

Jake had said little to Esther about Morrie since his Giants' debut. Except for a few nights when Morrie had been home and when the two men in her life were able to avoid each other because of their different hours, her son had been out of town. But every morning for the past few weeks, before Jake left for work, after carefully reading the paper with his bread and tea, he had reminded her not to throw it out or use it on the floors after she washed them.

"What for Jake?" she had complained the first time he asked. "I have enough shmootz to take care of around here."

Jake hadn't answered. He just gave her one of his stern looks that underlined the urgency of his request and went out the door. So she did what he asked, folding the *World* in quarters and piling them in chronological order on the shelf in his closet next to the bag that held his tallis. But not before she spent her own time with headlines and stories about their son.

Almost every day since Morrie left, his name appeared in the sportspages. "Ginsberg Quiets Cubs, Honored by Local Jewish Organizations," "Giants' Hebrew Handcuffs Phillies," and only today, "The Rabbi of Swat Swallows the Pirates, Lead Cut to Two,"—headlines about Morrie leaped out at Mama even if the details that followed were beyond her comprehension. Jake, too, read each word carefully. He didn't say anything to her about the stories but he spent more time on the sports page than anyplace else. And he never saved newspapers before.

Meanwhile Mama began to understand baseball. Essie Goldstein helped. Every morning, after her husband Max had left for work in the same tailor shop on Pitkin Avenue with Jake, Essie, a heavyset woman a little older than Mama and from the same town in Russia that Jake and Mama came from, came over for tea on her way to the stalls and street vendors on the Avenue where she did her daily shopping.

"Look at this, Esther," Essie bellowed one morning soon after Jake left. Essie didn't talk or speak—rather she proclaimed in a loud nasal way that demanded attention usually out of proportion with the importance of her words.

"Morrie is here in the *Forvetz*. It says that he is the new star of the Giants, a man that all Jews should be proud of and that he should be careful that the capitalists who pay his salary don't exploit him."

Esther heard all this as she poured tea for her friend and carried over the cups to the kitchen table where Essie sat. Setting down the cup, her eyes quickly scanned the familiar columns of Yiddish, her face in proud smile as she read the nice things that Abe Cahan had to say about her son.

What made her just as excited was a story that appeared next to the one on Morrie titled "The Fundamentals of Baseball Explained to Non-Sports," complete with a diagram of the Polo Grounds.

"An answer to a mother's prayers," she said, as she asked Essie if she could have the clipping. "Now, maybe I can understand better what this game is that Morrie plays."

Every morning since, before she put Jake's papers in the closet, Mama took out Cahan's story from her apron pocket, sat down with the sports pages, and began to learn about America's National Game and her son's occupation. By the time Morrie struggled past the Pirates by a 6–4 score, she understood the difference between the pitcher and the shortstop and no longer feared for her son's life when men with sticks stepped up to home plate. Although a sacrifice fly still meant no more to her than a suicide squeeze, she began to appreciate that the Giants were making a strong run for something called a pennant. Even without Cahan's help, she also knew, as she read in the paper, that Morrie and the Giants were due home in two days, in hot pursuit of the Pirates and three days before the start of Rosh Hashanah.

So did Jake. And not just from reading the papers. No matter where he went in the neighborhood, everyone stopped and asked about Morrie.

"I can't buy a paper or a piece of fruit even, without someone wanting to know about Morrie's arm, the score of the game, when he's coming home, what gifts he got where. It's meshugah," he complained to Max as the two men walked down Sackman Street and turned up Pitkin Avenue on their way to Mendelsohn's Tailors a few days after Morrie had left for Chicago.

"No one ever paid so much mind of me or Morrie before. It's like he's everybody's son now."

"So what's so bad, Jake?" Max inquired.

Jake shrugged his shoulders and remained silent—no answers now for the only man with whom he had ever come close to sharing any of his deepest feelings—even if the question cut him to the heart.

The two men walked on in silence; past the candy store, the butcher, and the fish store, pausing a moment to look at the fresh catch of flounder deposited on the crushed ice in the bins out front.

Then Jake broke the silence: "Any news about Shlomo? Will he be joining us for Rosh Hashanah?"

"I told you Jake, of him I no longer speak. He is dead to me." Max's response chilling the air once again.

"What about Morrie? will he be there?"

"I don't know Max. Who can keep track of his whereabouts these days? Chasing baseballs here and there! I'm sure he thinks he's much too important now to remember the New Year!"

But even as the words escaped his mouth, Jake felt that uncomfortable feeling deep in the pit of his soul. It wouldn't do to rant and rave about what a waste Morrie was making of his life or how he was the butt of that goyim McConnell's jokes. Even when he had hurt Morrie with such remarks, he couldn't deny the pride and love that had swelled up in his heart that afternoon at the Polo Grounds— feelings that he kept inside, to himself. Why so difficult to be honest about how he felt about his boy? Not a new question, but one more difficult than ever to repress.

[Excuse me, but are you sure you have your generations straight? Even Tevye as we know him best, Zero Mostel center stage on Broadway not Topol's luke-warm silver screen version, lacked the insight and introspection you expect from Jake. Maybe if he was Morrie twenty-five years later, a second-generation father doing battle with his Cold War baby boy—your Portnoy—you might have something. But is it fair to expect the same from some aging green-horn in 1927? And remember, I told you before, think of the children, not the fathers.]

Not that Esther gave him much choice. The very day she read in the papers that Morrie was coming home she began her campaign to reunite father and son in the warmth and spirit of the New Year. Even in the worst of times between Morrie and Jake, the High Holidays had offered a respite from the war of gestures and unspoken words that set the two men in her life at odds with each other. Whether it was the message of the days—its call for renewal, forgiveness, and community—or the accompanying festivities and ritual—from kreplach to Kol Nidre—Rosh Hashanah and Yom Kippur always seemed to be a healing time in her family. This year she knew the power of faith and tradition would truly be put to the test. It wouldn't hurt, she thought, to add her own two cents to whatever magic God might be able to work.

Esther launched her attack at dinner the very night Morrie descended on Squirrel Hill—over a meal of boiled flanken and fresh horseradish hot enough to sear whatever meat was still left on the boiled bones, a meal that was Jake's favorite and served only on special occasions or when overtime had been particularly good.

"So what should we do about Rosh Hashanah this year?" Mama asked Jake, as he sopped up the last drops of horseradish and gravy on his plate with a chunk of fresh rye bread.

"What's to do?" Jake responded. "I will go to Mendelsohn's only until 2, walk home with Max, go to shul at 7, come home at 9, and we'll eat with Max and Essie like always. You had something different in mind?"

"Not really. Only I was thinking. . . . Morrie will be back next week. I'm sure he will be coming home to celebrate with us but maybe we should send him a telegram and remind him just the same."

"Who died? A telegram? You want to scare him to death?" Jake groused, pushing his plate away to make room for the tea and sponge cake that Mama put down in front of him. "Besides, how do you know when Morrie is coming home? He hasn't written since he left."

"I read it in the paper, Jake, just like you," retorted Esther. "You think I don't know why you save the *World* every day."

"Me save the world? And every day! I didn't know I was so important!"

"Very funny, Jake, very funny."

"I only thought you were making a joke, in English no less."

"It's no joke. And to Moey, you are very important."

"All right, all right already. I'll send a telegram."

"Tomorrow?"

"Tomorrow, on the way home from work."

"Good Jake. And tell Moey that if he wants, he should bring some of his new friends home with him for dinner. It would be nice to fill up our table for the New Year."

"I will, Mama, I will."

◇

10

DORIS, TOO, KEPT her own collection. Not of Morrie's newspaper clippings but his letters; one written every day since he went on the road, the first one penned even before he left for Chicago, just as he promised, even though she told him that there was no point to it. Not that she didn't want to hear from him. What girl wouldn't jump at the chance to have someone personally verify the population and principal occupations of the people of three major cities! So she told Morrie on the phone the morning he left west; the morning after they spent most of the night driving around Manhattan and the Bronx before she dropped him off on Flatbush Avenue just over the bridge, just after their first and only kiss shyly offered by Morrie.

"It's just that it takes at least three days for a letter to arrive from Michigan. I'll be lucky if I receive half of what you write before you get back," she told him.

No matter. He wrote every day—about the weather, what he saw, Pullman trains, stockyard smells, city streets—a growing tapestry of new experience of which she was now a part. That's what he wrote. Not in so many words, but between the lines of his fountain pen scrawl written with a black, silver-tipped Parker that he received on his bar mitzvah from Max and Essie and that still worked to perfection, silver bar tilting up in blue-black ink bottle, sucking up lifeblood in a bubbling swirl that never ceased to amaze him.

And the mail worked better than Doris imagined. By the time Morrie set the Pirates down in order she had received five letters, each one on elegant hotel stationery—each one increasing her anticipation of the next—arriving with no regularity, once two at once and then nothing for three days, all delivered to Radio City to Doris Smith, care of the Rockettes. Even though she didn't read the sports pages, she, too, knew Morrie was due back in the city today. Every letter included that information; matter of factly stated in off-hand fashion—"Oh by the way, I will be back in New York sometime on Saturday, the 22nd," skip a line, "Morrie"—the message that closed every letter she received.

Doris hated Saturdays—a matinee followed by two evening shows. It didn't even pay to shower in between. Oh to be a Rockette—models of feminine beauty and beguiling grace in scant feather and silk. If only her adoring male audience could catch a whiff of the sweat of her real world, the one that served as everyone else's fantasy, the Music Hall would close its doors forever.

"Any mail today, Harry?" she asked the stage door attendant, as she headed back to the cattle-call dressing room she shared with twenty-five other shimmering, sweated beauties, each with their own dream of stardom, who came from all over the country to make their mark on the Great White Way.

"I already told you, Sweetie, there's only one delivery on Saturday and you weren't in it."

"So you did. Sorry, I forgot," Doris replied, not bothering to stop, surprised and excited by her desire for more of this man she hardly knew—who suddenly appeared before her at the door to her dressing-room, suitcase in hand, fresh off the train from Pittsburgh, awkwardly trying to avoid the crowd of dancers who rushed by him on the way to their dressing tables and toilets. Morrie's back was to her as she came up behind him. Quickly she turned him around, and without any warning of the sweaty realities of a dancer's life, she kissed him gently on the lips, cupping his face in her hands as he clung to his suitcase.

"Hello Morrie, I'm glad to see you again."

"Me too," he stumbled, face flushed by this unexpected but hoped for greeting. "I mean I'm glad to see you. Did you get any of my letters? I wrote every day."

"Yes I did. Five of them so far."

"There's more coming, but the last one I didn't send. I wrote it on the train this afternoon," he said, taking an envelope outside of his jacket pocket. "Is there some place I can read it to you?"

"Sure, we can go over here," Doris replied, taking Morrie by the hand and leading him to an open space across from her dressing room that contained a table, a few chairs, and a pay phone. "O.K., I'm all ears."

Morrie smiled nervously, sat down next to Doris, cleared his throat, and began to read:

———

Dear Doris,

I am sitting in the parlor car looking at the window. We just passed through Scranton, Pennsylvania: Population 43,000, settled by Moravians in 1735, principal industries: coal and steel. You can tell just by looking out the window, not the part about the Moravians, but the town is dotted with large smokestacks with black smoke constantly pouring out of their tops.

This morning before we left the hotel I got a telegram from my father who I haven't spoken to or heard from since I left New York. "Come home for the New Year," it read, "bring two friends." The New Year my father is talking about is the Jewish New Year. We call it Rosh Hashanah and we celebrate it this Monday night. I would be honored if you could be one of those friends he mentioned. I already invited Zack and he accepted. If you can't make it, though, I will understand.

———

"Is that the end?" Doris laughed nervously. "I've gotten used to more detailed descriptions of places and people. I really liked your letters."

"And this one?"

"I'm flattered to be asked, Morrie, really. But why me and Zack? You hardly know either one of us. Are we what your father had in mind as 'friends'?"

Morrie laughed when he thought of Zack. As much as he worried about his own meeting with his father, he could hardly wait for Esther and Jake to meet his new Giant companion. Maybe they could figure out this Southern catcher whose grasp of Yiddish and love of Jewish delicacies was almost as good as his own.

"For your information, Zack was thrilled with the invitation. He's been salivating over the prospects of pot roast, chopped liver, kreplach and chicken soup since I asked him if he could come. In fact, he's going to shul with me and my father before we go home to eat. To tell you the truth, sometimes I wonder if he might be Jewish. And I like him."

"Shul? kreplack? I think I need a translation!"

"Or at least a lesson in pronunciation! Come on Monday and you'll see. That's your night off, isn't it?"

"Yes, but . . . I don't know Morrie. I don't see where I fit into all this."

Morrie, who had been standing since he began his recitation, sat down in the chair next to Doris and took her hand in his. "Look Doris," he began, "I don't have any exact answer for you. All I know is that since I met you I haven't been able to get you out of my mind. I just want to spend more time with you and see what happens."

Doris squeezed Morrie's hand tenderly. "Morrie, I've been thinking about you too. And I do want to see you again. I'm just not so sure that going to your parents to dinner on such a special day is such a good idea. After all my name is Smith. Jesus Christ," she laughed, "my mother's ancestors came over on the *Mayflower*! What would your father think of that?"

Morrie laughed. "I agree it would be easier if you had a less obvious Protestant name . . . something vaguely Russian might be nice. Look, why don't I wait for you here while you change. Then I'll walk you home, if that's all right with you. We can figure this out together."

"I can't. I have another show to do at 9."

"That's O.K. I've never been to Radio City before. What if I buy a ticket, see the show, and meet you back here when it's over?"

"Why not?" Doris replied. "But only if you promise to tell me more about Scranton."

"All that your heart desires."

SATURDAY NIGHTS AT the Blossom Heath were always hot, whether or not the Babe was in attendance. But this one was special. The Yankee slugger had been on a tear, crushing his fifty-seventh home run that very afternoon as his teammates clinched their fifth pennant since 1921. And they all came to the inn to celebrate, everyone, that is, with the exception of Lou Gehrig who begged off to be with his mother in the Bronx.

By the time Zack Taylor pulled into the parking lot, Benny and Babe had already entertained the crowd. Even Miller Huggins joined in, bounding up on the stage at the Babe's invitation where he proceeded to offer toast upon toast to every Yankee player, punctuating each one by putting his fist through his already crushed Panama and leading his boys in several choruses of "Roll Out the Barrel," triumphant Yankee ritual shared by all.

"Good evening, Zack," David Weiss, formally attired as always in black tie, greeted the Giant catcher. "An odd night for you to be here, but as always a pleasure to see you. Will you be dining alone?"

"Actually, Mr. Weiss, I came to talk to you, when you have a moment." Catching the maître d's puzzled look, Zack smiled. "Don't worry, it's nothing serious. I just need your advice about a little matter and I think you might be able to help me."

"Sure, Zack, sure. It's pretty busy now but let me get you seated and I'll come back when I can." With that Weiss checked his table chart, beckoned Zack to follow him, and led him off to a little table left of main stage against the side wall of the inn. "This is as quiet as it's going to get in here tonight. Enjoy your meal and I'll return when I can."

"I've already eaten. Just have a waiter send over something to drink. But it is a meal that I want to talk to you about. I'll see you later."

A confused Weiss drifted back into the melee of party-goers while Taylor surveyed the house, looking for familiar Giant faces that he hoped to avoid. Not that he was likely to find any in a sea of Yankee players and well-wishers, especially since the Giants hadn't arrived at Grand Central until 6:30 P.M. Everyone he talked to on the long ride from Pittsburgh had only one thing in mind at the end of a tiring but successful road trip—their own bed and a good night's sleep. Everyone, that is, except Morrie who, Zack knew, was by now at Radio City inviting Doris to a New Year's celebration—the same invitation that had made him unintended witness to this scene of Yankee revelry.

Assured of his anonymity, Zack leaned his chair against the wall and let his eyes close, the moment immediately shattered by a voice familiar to anyone who spent much time at the Blossom Heath or who knew anything about baseball.

"So deep in thought on a night like this? C'mon keed, join the party!" This from the man of the hour who recognized the Giant catcher off by himself on his way back from the men's room.

"Thanks Babe, but I prefer to sit this one out. Besides it wouldn't be right to get too close to you guys. After all, in a few weeks we might be ferrying across the Harlem to play each other."

"I prefer the 155th Street bridge," Ruth laughed. "Did you ever see all the shit that floats down the river? Reminds me of the Baltimore docks when I still lived at home. We'd swim off the pier all the time, just like the kids do from the rocks in front of the stadium. Never thought twice about all that scum that passed for water. Now, I wouldn't risk such harm to this beautiful and famous body."

"You're right, Babe, clearly an unnecessary risk. Hey, congratulations on your 57th. Only three more to go!"

"Yeah," Ruth said, pulling out a chair from the table, turning it around in one hand and sitting down, his forearms resting on its back as he leaned in to face Zack. "But you would hardly know it from the papers. First time in a while that I can remember more coverage of Giant road games and rookie pitchers than the exploits of the Great Bambino and Murderer's Row. Is this Greenstein as good as they say he is?"

"It's Ginsberg, Babela, not Greenstein, and you know it wouldn't be kosher for me to tell you much. After all, with any luck he'll be pitching against you in no time."

"What's this Babela crap, Zack? You a Yid too?"

"Sorry, Babe. I didn't mean anything by it. I guess the kid's rubbing off on me. We room together on the road. Everywhere we go, Jews follow him around and offer him gifts, sometimes even their daughters. I guess I just picked up some of their lingo."

"Their daughters, huh?" Babe paused, pondering the possibilities. "You know I met the boy here about a month ago. He seemed real nervous but from the way he's been winning I guess he's settled down."

"I was here that night you rescued Morrie from Whiteman and Hornsby. I know he appreciated the assist."

"Tell him the pleasure was all mine, from one Sultan to another, if you know what I mean. And tell him I hope to meet him again in the Series. He can repay the favor with a few nice pitches right down the middle. I'll just let you know when I'm ready and you can signal the boy to oblige."

Babe laughed as he stood up from the table, mimicking, with his right arm the height and position of his favorite home run pitch. "After all, Rabbis, I mean, Sultans, are made, not born."

"O.K., Babe," Zack replied, standing up to shake the slugger's hand. "I'll see what I can do, if we get that far. In the meantime, although I know I don't have to tell you, enjoy the evening."

Zack returned to his seat as Babe moved through a crowd of backslapping well-wishers who stood up from their tables or stopped in their tracks to congratulate and touch their hero as he made his way to his own table across the room.

"Are you and Mr. Taylor finished with your conversation, Babe?" David Weiss asked, as the Yankee slugger passed by. Playfully, Babe swung his huge arm over Weiss's diminutive shoulders, engulfing the maître d' in a bear-hug and whispered in the affirmative.

Unnoticed to them all were three other men, precisely dressed in dark pinstripes seated at a table no more than fifteen feet to the left of Zack's—in subtle contrast to the dinner-jacketed, tuxedoed bodies of the party-goers that dominated the crowd. Neither invited participants to Yankee celebration nor aware of Zack's planned visit, they had arrived at the Inn after concluding their own business on Long Island. Shikey Friedman insisted. After all, Brooklyn gangsters out to gauge the possibilities of moving their protection racket to new turf deserved a chance to celebrate the prospects and catch a meal on the way back home.

Friedman had been the first to spot Taylor and Ruth sitting together. Everyone knew the Babe, but Friedman had been a big Giants' rooter for years. He had always made good book on McGraw's team and enjoyed watching the game at the Polo Grounds, even if his own playing days behind the plate ended in the schoolyard at P.S. 184 when easy money and fast women became more powerful attractions. Taylor had always been one of his favorite players ever since he came to the club in 1920. He had been impressed with how the big catcher had handled his old childhood acquaintance only a few weeks before. No more than a minute after he pointed out Zack's presence to Izzy Cohen and Fats Goldstein, Ruth had joined the Giants catcher. And now, as Friedman noticed, David Weiss had taken his place.

"So my friend, how can I be of service? Is it a matter of what spoon to use or where to place your water glass that brings you to my inn?"

"No Davey," Zack smiled as Weiss took the Babe's vacated seat. "Etiquette is not the issue, at least not the knives and forks variety. Monday night, Morrie Ginsberg invited me to his house for Rosh Hashanah. He even asked me to go with him and his father to synagogue before the meal."

"So?"

"So? So I'm not sure what to do. I thought maybe you could offer some counsel."

Weiss listened carefully, motioned Taylor to him, leaned over the table and quietly whispered, "Just continue your charade of the Southern yokel and no one will be the wiser. It worked in Chicago, and it's been working here, so what's the problem?"

"The problem is that it's not so easy any more. Ten years ago it seemed like the only thing to do if I ever wanted to get a chance to play in the bigs. No one ever gave me a serious look when I was Philly Schwartz. Even McGraw hadn't yet begun his search for Jewish talent to challenge the Babe. My God, Ruth was still in a Baltimore orphan's home. So I used what I learned from watching my parents on the vaudeville circuit. I nurtured my Southern accent, made sure to shower after everyone had left the clubhouse so no one would see my circumcised cock, and transformed myself from a Hebrew pariah into what you know and love today—a talented catcher with a Southern drawl who inadvertently drops Yiddish phrases, puzzles the shit out of his new Jewish roommate, and constantly questions exactly who he is and where he fits."

"Again, I repeat, so what's the problem." Just as if he was explaining the difference between the way his chefs prepared filet mignon or Beef Wellington to a first-time customer, Weiss continued: "It seems to me you have two choices. Continue as Zack Taylor, the goy who somehow knows enough about Jewish custom to keep his roommate guessing. Or let everyone know that you're really a nice Jewish boy from Tallahassee named Philly Schwartz. Take the first option and its only your inner anguish that's the issue. Cleanse your soul of repression and guilt and who knows what will happen."

"I'm not sure I caught the last part," Zack replied, leaning back in his chair as Weiss stood up, his hands now resting on the edge of the table.

"All I mean, Zack, is that once you reveal your true identity, there's no way to be sure how the press will handle it or what they will ask you. Why did you change your name? Are baseball players anti-Semite bastards? And who knows how your teammates might respond or how it might affect the end of the season. I don't have to tell you about the delicate chemistry on a baseball team. Ginsberg has been a spark for you boys. But two Hebrews on the same team! Then again. . . . But don't tell me you didn't think of all this yourself."

"Not quite in so many words. That's why I wanted to run it by you. Ever since you helped me out in Chicago, you've always been a friend whose opinion I value."

Weiss's face reddened. "There is no need to bring up Chicago."

"But if you hadn't tipped me off to Gandil's scheme, God knows what. . . ."

"That was another lifetime ago, Zack. Please, let's forget it."

Not that Weiss ever could. He had been in charge of the dining room of the Broadmoor Hotel where Taylor frequently ate, when the rookie catcher sought him out, sensing something wrong with the play of some of his teammates in the second game of the World Series with Cincinnati. Taylor had known Weiss from his Catskills childhood; accompanying his parents each summer as they traipsed from Kiamesha Lake to Loch Sheldrake catering to the garish tastes of Jewish vacationers from Brooklyn and the Bronx, while Weiss made sure that there was enough lox and herring available for breakfast in his dining room at the Concord. And he had given him good advice. Keep your mouth shut, he told him. You're not likely to catch and you can't prove anything. Right on both counts and Zack had escaped the scandal without a mention. No one, certainly not Zack, knew the full story behind Weiss's connection to the Black Sox scandal, but now, eight years later, he recognized that he had brought immediate and uncomfortable memories to the surface.

"I didn't mean anything by it, Davey. It's just that I trust your opinion. I just wanted to make sure that I had covered all the bases before I decided what to do."

Recovered now, Weiss stood up and patted Taylor on the shoulder. "You flatter me, my friend. With a mind like yours, there's not a chance that you wouldn't." Bowing his head in farewell, the master of the house returned to the bustle of the Blossom Heath, a gesture acknowledged both by a relaxed smile by the Giant catcher and by the intent stare of the Jewish gangster whose attention had been fixed on the pair from the moment they began to converse.

———————

———

Shikey Friedman barely spoke on the way back to Brownsville. Alone in the backseat of Cohen's Studebaker roadster, oblivious to the banter of his two friends as they debated the merits of the Blossom Heath's menu, he conjured up the conversations he had just witnessed. Taylor and Ruth, Ruth and Weiss, Weiss and Taylor—not that any of the combinations was necessarily odd or out of place— certainly not at the Inn. Rather, the coincidence of their occurrence fueled his imagination. Prohibition and protection offered their own rewards—steady income, a chance to show a little muscle, easy lays, plenty of time to fuck off at the track or the pool room. But Shikey always wanted something more; something big and flashy, done on his own terms that would make everyone sit up and take notice; not just local neighborhood punks but the big kikes and wops, men like Rothstein and Capone who ran the show and parceled out the daily work that kept him and his boys in the black. An opportunity of his own creation more and more had preoccupied him; forged from everyday event and circumstance, providing catapult beyond his circumscribed criminal world and the confines of Brownsville—a world of two-bit hoodlums, penny-ante prostitutes, deadly familiar faces and streets—one with which he grew increasingly impatient. Tonight, however, the abstract, for the first time, became concrete.

As Izzy steered his Studebaker off the Sunrise Highway onto Linden Road headed towards Pitkin Avenue, Friedman broke his own silence.

"Izzy, how long has David Weiss been at the Blossom Heath?"

Cohen, a good ten years older than Friedman, heavy-set at six feet and 230 pounds, who enjoyed his role as chauffeur almost as much as he relished the crunch of his brass knuckles against the jawbone of a reluctant "client," answered in his usual staccato voice, "Five years, maybe six. Came from Chicago. Rothstein set him up. Owns half of the inn himself."

Full of a still adolescent enthusiasm, especially for accomplishments that he never hoped to match, Fats Goldstein added his own contribution:

"Yeah, some sort of payback for his work in pulling off the World Series scam. Boy, that was a piece of work! Wasn't he the guy who tipped Rothstein off about Attell and Sullivan?"

"That's what I know," Friedman continued. "Weiss worked at the Broadmoor where the White Sox often dined. He sensed something was up when Abe Attell and Joey Sullivan started showing up on a regular basis a few weeks before the World Series. It was not big news that the Chicago players had had it with Comiskey. He paid them peanuts while they produced pennants. Then Joe Jackson confided in Weiss. The poor shmuck! My guess is that he got a bum rap when they threw him out of the game. Anyway, once Weiss figured out what was going on, he tipped off Rothstein. Arnold took it from there, laid off his bets, and walked away leaving Attell and Sullivan holding the bag."

"If you already knew this, then why the question?" Goldstein asked.

Friedman leaned forward and playfully cuffed Fats in the head. "Because, my friend, tonight at the Inn I got the beginnings of an idea that may make us all rich and famous. Does your father still work with Jake Ginsberg?"

"Yeah, they're best of friends. But what's the connection between them and your 'idea.'"

"I don't know for sure yet, Fats, I don't know. But watching Zack Taylor tonight with Ruth and then Weiss got me thinking about 1919. Nobody's pulled anything like that off since. But maybe we have something special to play with, all of us knowing Morrie so well...."

"Careful, Shikey, careful. Risky business, baseball," Izzy intoned from the front, his eyes fixed straight ahead, as the car sped across Nostrand Avenue, past the new Loew's movie theatre, just now emptying out its Saturday night crowd. "Even Rothstein stays away. You want sports, stay with boxers. Easy to rig. No one gives a shit. Besides, if it couldn't be done with eight players, how to do it with one pitcher?"

"That's what makes it so enticing, Izzy. No one would expect any one to fuck around again. No one would think any player would be stupid enough to put their career on the line for a few extra bucks, not after what happened to the White Sox. Not the public. Not even Arnold. I don't even know yet how or if we can pull it off. We just need to think about it, that's all."

12

"THINK ABOUT IT ESTHER," Jake growled as he stepped out of his slippers and climbed into the narrow double bed that he shared with his wife, his feet still white with talcum powder, too freely sprinkled after his bath. "Morrie invites two goyim to dinner who he hardly knows—one a shiksa no less, and the other a Southern boy who wants to go to shul with me for Rosh Hashanah. What's he trying to do, kill me?"

"Ssh Jakie," Esther murmured, pressing her ample body against her husband's side and running her fingers through the bushy, black hair on his chest. "Moey is a good boy. He means no harm. Just try to enjoy his good fortune. I don't know anything about his friends, but if Moey likes them, how bad can they be? You'd have plenty to complain about if he had turned out like Shlomo Goldstein."

"Is that goniff coming Tuesday? Max never talks about him. I asked him but he said nothing."

"I don't ask. If he comes, he comes. Maybe it would do him good to talk to Moey. They used to be such good friends when they were little."

"My son the messiah," Jake sighed. "Only in this country could such a thing happen. A boy throws a ball for a few hours twice a week and makes more money than his father who sweats away fifty hours making fancy woolen pants for rich people on Park Avenue."

Esther laughed softly, pressing her head into Jake's chest, her hands moving down to untie the draw strings on his pajama bottoms, drifting still further in slow, circular motions of arousal. "So what's so terrible that a son should do better than his father?" she whispered. "Isn't that why you came to America in the first place?"

"Please Esther, not now. Let us not lose this moment," Jake groaned, his penis growing limp in the face of Morrie's intrusion into even these most intimate of places.

Esther recognized her error and reclaimed the night with her hands. Which Jake appreciated, even as he recognized in the instant that what she said was true, abstractly always, and in the beginning, especially. But years of dreary tailoring, the simple grind of daily life, the natural tension of generations at odds with each other over everyday matters of what should be simple, taken-for-granted things—what language to speak, what food to eat, or what to do for a living—all took their toll. In such a world, a son's joyous enthusiasm and obvious talent nurtured by a mother's love became barriers to a father's love and hopes. But here, caught in the ecstasy of a singular moment between Esther and himself, something special and their own, Jake moaned in appreciation of his wife's diligence in bringing his largeness back and for reminding him of his son.

———————————

———

[Jewish sex is something! Now don't get me wrong. I mean nothing anti-Semitic here. But when I got it on, I got it on, if you know what I mean. Shit, there was no time for such deep reflection and catharsis! Especially when I was with more than one woman at the same time. Which happened a lot, believe me! Well, not quite the way that story goes, you know the one. When was it, 1930, '31? I had a roommate on the Yankees named Jimmy Reese. He's still around, in his 90s now, and the last time I looked some kind of coach with the California Angels—Jewish to boot. Anyway, one of his jobs as a utility man was to make sure I got to the ballpark ready to play. One time, as the story goes, I lock him out of our hotel room—I can't remember what town we were in—while I got it on with six "annies," with a break for a fresh cigar in between innings, if you know what I mean. Finally, his own job on the line, Jimmy breaks into the room to hustle me to the ballpark. Supposedly I turn to him, exhausted, and say: What took you so long, kid?—five cigar butts in my ashtray and a fresh panatela in my mouth. The fact was that it was only three, but let me tell you, it was all business. Focused concentration on the moment at hand, that's the key, whatever the balls!]

———————————

———

The Babe was not so lucky. Not that he hadn't chosen wisely from the abundant offerings at the Blossom Heath. Daisy, she called herself, like the character in some guy's new novel that someone told her about, she said—big-breasted, the way he liked his women, inviting, full, red-lipsticked lips that excited his imagination as much as the black silk that wrapped around her tightly-packed body—all told a perfect way to end a pennant-clinching celebration, or for that matter, any day for the Great Bambino. Or so he thought as they motored back to the Alamac at 1 A.M.

Three hours later, his room in typical disarray—half-eaten plates of prime rib precariously balanced on a room service cart still with its unlit candles no longer erect in their holders, his clothes strewn all about, bedspreads and blankets pushed to the floor from the evening's encounter—Babe was not so sure. At issue was not the state of his quarters but the limp member between his legs as he lay in bed, curled up like an unborn baby, his head propped up against the pillows.

It had been twenty minutes since Daisy left, sworn to secrecy about the fact that the Sultan of Swat had struck out without a swing.

"Don't worry, honey," she told him, climbing back into her dress after all of her best efforts had failed to bring him around. "Even you can't expect to hit a home run every time you step up to the plate."

"Not a word about this, right, Daisy?"

"Sure thing, Babe. Your secret's safe with me. Will I see you again?"

"Sure kid, I'll catch you at the Inn next week."

At least she knows her baseball, Ruth mused as she closed the door behind her. But what the fuck was up, he wondered. Certainly not the Babe. "Shit, I don't understand it. What the hell is going on here?" he rasped.

Ruth rolled out of bed and lumbered towards the bathroom. He stepped into the shower, turned on the hot and cold spigots full blast, allowing the water to explode across his face and chest in hope of revival. Standing there, water cascading over him, Babe ran through the evening, searching for a clue to his misadventure in the evening's celebration. It couldn't have been the booze, nothing unusual there. Maybe he ate something that didn't agree with him. No, that never stopped him before. Shit, the only thing out of the ordinary had been finding Taylor there on the night the Yankees won the pennant. Nothing there, just some chatter about dirty water and that Jew pitcher, Babe shrugged.

"At least I'm still hitting the ball," he thought, stepping out of the shower and wrapping himself in the oversized terrycloth robe that the hotel provided. Toweling off his penis, now surprisingly large and firm in his own hands, he laughed out loud about the evening's misadventure, thought first of Daisy, whose name still lingered in his memory, and then of the last woman he hadn't done it with—not because he wasn't able but because she had told him to fuck off. "What the hell was her name?" he wondered, "not Daisy but something with a D, a dancer too with the Rockettes. Maybe I should give her another try."

Babe climbed back into bed, mind calm but appetites aroused, but too early even for the ever-obedient Alamac staff to bring up his usual morning fare. Taking matters into his own hands, Babe satisfied himself, thinking both of Daisy and the rockette, what the hell did she call herself—"Doris!" he ejaculated, "that's her name!"

"Doris, that's right, her name is Doris, Ma. I'll come by the house with her around 5:30 and then Pa, me, and my friend Zack, will go to shul. Doris says she'll be glad to help. O.K., see you tomorrow."

"I don't know about this," Doris sighed, taking the phone from Morrie and replacing it in the cradle on her side of her bed.

Morrie, freshly showered, his hair still damp, rolled over in the narrow bed, took Doris' hand in his own and leaned back on the pillows, surveying her one bedroom, three story walk-up, Christopher Street flat as the morning sun streaked in from the east. The bed took up much of the room, a white ceilinged, blue-painted walled rectangle otherwise occupied by a dresser, two small night tables, a floor lamp and a rocking chair where, he marveled, lay his virgin pants and underwear. "That's what I said last night when you brought me back here," Morrie reminded her, "but everything turned out all right."

"These are not exactly parallel situations Morrie, at least for me. I don't need to meet your mother to sleep with you."

"It will be fine, you'll see."

"You keep on saying that, but I don't understand why. I mean, when was the last time you brought home a girl who wasn't Jewish."

"Actually, you're the first girl I've ever brought home."

"I'm flattered, really, but you're avoiding me. Look," Doris pleaded, "you're in enough hot water already with your father. Why not wait a while and see how things. . . ."

But Morrie was too buoyant, too hopeful, too full of himself and his new world of possibilities to fear the past's looming presence. . . .

"It will be alright, I'm telling you," he softly insisted, turning towards Doris, taking her hand to his mouth and kissing it gently.

Doris smiled into his eyes.

"Then you'll come tomorrow?"

"Alright already, I'll come, I'll come," Doris replied, trying her best to imitate the heavy, nasal, Jewish voices she heard every day on New York streets.

[Everybody's cumming, one way or another! I like that. Even Morrie, and so soon. No pun intended. Some literary effete might rag you here—not enough character development, too sudden a transformation from the shy, unskilled, clammy-handed boy of the Blossom Heath to Sackman Street Don Juan. But why not, heh? (I mean cumming not punning). Passion of the moment, cathartic departure from the past, that's what we should be thinking about, right? Hell. The kid's breathing the cock jock air of the celebrity ballplayer. Shit! Maybe's he thinking of me! Oh, by the way, in case anyone's keeping score, I always got it up!]

———————————

———

Morrie got out of bed, pulled on his pants, all the while laughing at her Jewish accent. "That's good enough for me. Look, I've got to get to the ballpark. Tomorrow, we have off. The Yankees are playing an early game at 1:00 at the Stadium that Zack and me are going to see. Then we'll come by Radio City and pick you up around 4:00 like we said."

Doris joined Morrie at the door, pulled his face down to hers, pushed her tongue through his unresisting lips and kissed him. "Fine Morrie, I'll be there with bells on."

Morrie smiled, closed the door behind him and headed down the stairs, lightheaded in the joyous freedom of the moment and surprised at how calm and confident he was the morning after losing his virginity with a blond-haired, beautiful shiksa, only a few days before he would pitch against the Cubbies in the heat of a season-ending tight race for the pennant and only a few hours before he was to take two goyim to have dinner with his parents on Rosh Hashanah!

"Oy, what a time," he laughed. No mimickry here, the words and inflection naturally rolling from his lips.

13

SOLEMNLY, CAREFULLY, Esther and Essie spread the white linen tablecloth over the kitchen table, the same one they used every year. Priestesses with holy water, each, then, took a handful of flour and sprinkled it evenly over the cloth—a fine white cloud of dust settling down in preparation for the ritual at hand. Starting from the middle of the table, they plied into a huge mound of white dough that Esther had prepared before breakfast, before Jake had left for work. Silently, diligently, they worked it over, spreading it thinner and thinner until it eventually covered the floured cloth in a thin uneven-edged wafer-thin layer, leaving only enough room at two corners for pots of cooked chop meat and cleaver-minced onions that sat cooling on the stove next to a huge pot full of water, onions, dill, celery, carrots and a chicken, quartered, plucked and cleaned the night before—all coming together into a rich broth that would be tomorrow evening's second course. Already Esther had roasted the yellow eggs pulled from the chicken's insides, one of Morrie's favorite treats. Later, when the soup was done, she would take the chicken skin and fry it up in its own fat, just the way he liked it.

Every year since they both moved to Sackman Street, Esther and Essie cooked together for the High Holidays, taking turns in each other's kitchens, preparing soup, kreplach, potato latkes, tzimmis, and brisket—perennial, unalterable, menu passed from generation to generation, brought to America from the Russian shtetls of their childhood. This year was no different, at least as far as the food was concerned.

"Do you think this Doris will like our food?" Essie asked, plopping teaspoons of meat onto the dough, then, with a sharp knife, cutting through it around each pile, just enough marked off to form small rectangles of meat-filled dough, pinched together at the top and ready for boil.

"It is the least of me what she likes," Esther growled, her own hands busy at the same task—each woman working quickly from opposite ends of the table towards the center, never missing a beat no matter their words.

"Morrie bringing home a shiksa, who would have thought it! But look at my Shlomo. Bums for friends! God knows what he does!"

"Is he coming tomorrow?"

"Ach, only God knows that too," Essie moaned. "Not a word from him in six months. For Max, he is dead."

Then only silence—except for the quick, slicing sounds of metal blades against the wooden table-top—each mother artfully plying her craft surrounded by familiar smells of simmering broth and cooked meat.

"So. What does Morrie say about this girl?" Essie asked, carrying the balls of dough and meat back to the stove and placing them in a pot of boiling water.

"Say?"

"Where does she live? What does she look like?" Essie elaborated, returning to the table with a glass of tea.

"Me you're asking? Who knows. All I know is that Moey invited this Doris Smith and a friend, his catcher, from the baseball team to come," Esther replied, sitting down now for the first time all morning, her white-floured hands stilled in her aproned lap. "We will see for yourself, tomorrow."

Essie laughed, playfully stirring her spoon around the sugar cube that bobbed up and down in her glass.

"Nu, did I make a joke?" Esther inquired abruptly.

"No, I'm sorry to laugh. It's just that your English is not always so. . . ."

"And you, The Perfect American! Is that such a wonderful thing to be?"

Silence again, two old friends embarrassed by themselves and their outbursts. . . .

————————

———

[My mother spoke good English. Not that she talked much. Not to me. I don't really remember that much about her. Shit, I was in the streets or at St. Mary's most of the time except when I was a little kid and that was too long ago to recall. When she wasn't working in the bar she was upstairs taking care of the other kids. But every once in a while, when things were going OK downstairs, she'd put on her best dress and coat and head uptown to shop. Sometimes she'd bring home a ribbon for my sister or some candy for me. Once, even, a new shirt for my father. And then she would cook. Not the everyday fare of bread and cabbage soup of questionable means concocted from her pushcart purchases on the docks, but red meat bought from a butcher, who, dressed in his white apron, proudly displayed his offerings in a glass case, like so many jewels—or so she told us. Corned beef, roasted potatoes, brown gravy, baked rolls slothed in butter, green beans and bacon. On those occasions, she made us all wash and dress as best as we could. It was worth it.]

"Good, tomorrow night you'll go eat at Ginsberg's house," Shikey Friedman instructed Fats, as they sat across from each other at Friedman's kitchen table, three stories up a brownstone, in front of a window that looked out on the school yard of P.S. 184, where boys jumped on each other, Johnny-on-the-pony against school yard fences clanging in harmony with the rock-tossing hops and skips of their sisters deep in their recess games of potsy.

Shikey certainly could have afforded better digs. His wardrobe underscored the possibility—a closetful of expensive, hand-tailored suits each with matching, well-shined Italian shoes and the appropriate tie and shirt. But he had vowed to himself that only after he hit it big on his own would he move out of Brooklyn; uptown—the West Side—and surround himself with the luxury that would mark his success. Never, he was sure, was he closer to it since he saw Taylor, Weiss and the Babe at the Blossom Heath.

"That won't be easy for me," whined Fats. "I haven't seen my parents for a year. To my father, I am dead. Why should I go?"

"Very simple," Shikey replied, patting Goldstein lightly in the face. "I have a plan and you going to dinner is part of it. Are you paying attention Izzy?"

Annoyed by the interruption, Izzy Cohen glanced over the top of the racing form he had been reading across the room, back to the wall, knees up on Friedman's bed, and nodded in the affirmative.

"Good. Now this all depends on the Giants winning the pennant. Not a sure thing I know, but they have been on a roll and Pittsburgh has been fading. Anyway, here it is. First, Fats, it is perfect that you have been on the outs with your parents. Because tomorrow night you will repent. What better time of year to do so? Surprise your father. Go to shul. Tell him that you have come to your senses. No more fucking around! No more muscling people or running around with those paskudynaks and shmucks you once called your friends. Tell him you have dishonored him. Tell him you want to make amends. Tell him you're Shlomo again. You'll go back to school. Maybe CCNY. Become a teacher. Make him proud. You know better than I what will work with him."

"Yeah," Izzy sneered. "Tell him his good, little Jew boy—fat little Shlomo—has come home for good."

"Shut your fuckin' mouth, Izzy! Jesus fucking Christ! How many times do I have to tell you? Lay off the kid!"

"Alright, alright Shikey. Fatsy here knows I was only kidding. Right, Fatsy?"

Red-faced, angry and frightened, Goldstein said nothing, his eyes focused on Friedman.

"Alright! Enough!" Shikey demanded, now across the room to

the straight-backed red leather chair over which his suit jacket lay draped. Reaching into the coat's inside pocket, he pulled out an overstuffed, sealed envelope, and with a flourish, placed it in Goldstein's hands.

"Open it."

"Holy shit! World Series tickets—third base boxes at the Stadium and the Polo Grounds for the last five games. How did you get them? The Giants haven't even won the pennant yet."

"Don't you read the papers?" Cohen digged. "Three weeks ago the National League told both the Pirates and the Giants to print tickets in advance, just in case. The Yankees probably made theirs up in May."

"Right," Shikey added. "Now, here's what I figured. I checked over the Giants' pitching rotation since Ginsberg came up. McGraw's a creature of habit. He's been using the kid as a spot starter, but on a regular basis. So, it comes down to every fifth day. Barring odd shit like playoffs or Morrie's arm falling off, if the Giants make it to the Series he'll probably get two starts—the third game at the Polo Grounds, and the seventh game, if it gets that far, at the Stadium. By the time he tows the rubber he'll be ours."

For once Izzy and Fats were on the same page. But before they could raise their confused voices demanding clarification and connection between Fats' homecoming and fixing the World Series, Shikey cut them off:

"I know, I know. I need to fill in the details. It's really pretty simple. Fats, you're going to take your father and Jake Ginsberg to the World Series with these tickets. But unfortunately, you take a few wrong turns in the Bronx and end up near the warehouse off Mosholu Parkway. And there, we kidnap all of you. Jake becomes our trump card. Morrie will do what we say or else we threaten to kill him. And you, Fats, and your father, add an additional touch of sincerity. You'll have to play your part good. Izzy here may have to slap you around a bit to make it stick—but it will be worth it."

"Wait a minute," Izzy finally intruded. "While I don't mind roughing up Fatsy here a bit, we have no more than ten days to set this up and only one rookie pitcher to count on to try to fix the World Series! They couldn't pull it off in 1919 with a lot more time and most of the fucking White Stockings in the bag!"

"That was the problem. Too much time for too much to go wrong—too many ballplayers and thieves involved to guarantee anything. Here it's simple. We don't try to fix the whole Series, only a few games. If it gets to the seventh game, then we stand to make a fortune. If not, there's still a big killing. We count on the most important player to pull it off and we leverage him, not with the promise of hard cash but with his father's life."

Fats shifted nervously in his chair. "But where do we get the money, Shikey? Even if we pulled this off, we don't have enough cash to hit it big."

"A good question, Shlomo, and not the only one, I imagine, that's on your mind. We could go to Rothstein. He's still 'the bankroll.' But then it wouldn't be ours anymore. Besides, the Yankees will be heavy favorites, especially against a rookie. I figure we need $50,000, carefully placed. More than that gets involved, and everyone will smell a fix. Right now I have about $2,000 stashed away. With collections from the next week we can bring in another $5,000. We just hold off giving it to Arnold—tell him people were late with their payments, and lay it off. So we're looking at about $40,000."

"That's still a chunk."

"I know, I know! But I also know where we'll get it. Davey Weiss is the key. That inn turns over a pretty penny every week. We also know that Weiss bought into that place with the money he made off helping Rothstein fix the 1919 series. Everyone in New York knows that the Blossom Heath is where the Yankees and the Giants hang out. All we do is threaten Weiss with spilling the beans about what he did in Chicago, couple it with rumors about his plan to try it again this year in New York, and he'll roll over for us. Whether he remortgages the place or borrows from his partners, he'll come up with the money. While you, Fats, transform yourself back into obedient Jew, Izzy and I will have a little chat with our Mr. Weiss."

Izzy smiled at the prospect. Fats, on the other hand, was less certain about his own. Fats never questioned or challenged Shikey. After all, this friend from school yard days took him in after he quit high school, after his father threw him out of the house—fed and clothed him, gave him a chance to make good money, far more than his father ever saw—made him feel important—made him part of a new life full of freedom and excitement far bigger than what Essie and Max offered him in their familiar, stifling Sackman Street world.

But these new marching orders chilled him. Returning to his father's fold, even as part of a scam, would be hard enough on him. Besides, how could Shikey be sure that his father would even talk to him, let alone believe him? And if he did, what would happen to Jake Ginsberg and his father after they had been kidnapped?

"I don't know," Fats began, but before he could voice his fears, Shikey intervened.

"Look, Fatsy, I know you can do this. I have faith in you. Don't worry about your father. Go to shul. Go to dinner at the Ginsbergs.

Trust me, your father will give you another chance. He has no choice. And don't worry. No one is going to get hurt. There won't be any rough stuff. We just hold you all until it's over and then everyone goes home."

"But what happens then? How are you gonna keep Ginsberg or my father from going to the cops? What am I supposed to do when he finds out that I was involved?"

"Easy, real easy. First of all, no one is likely to believe the cockamamy story they might tell. And just in case, we make it clear that if they even think about it, someone could get hurt. As for you," Shikey added in a quiet but firm voice, now standing in front of his seated soldier, hands firmly clasped on Fats's shoulders, "What the fuck do you care what your father thinks? Enjoy the opportunity to screw him for thinking of you dead!"

Shlomo didn't move, chin pressed against his chest.

Gently, Shikey chucked him on the chin and lifted his face towards his. "Don't worry, Fatsy. Have I ever steered you wrong? This will be alright. You can count on it. Come'n. Let's go to the park and shoot some baskets. Five dollars a letter for HORSE. What'dya say?"

This time Shlomo nodded his head up and down.

◇

14

HEADS BOBBING UP and down, a cacophony of movement in rhythm with the individual chants of forty or so men standing in front of wooden benches before a simple, raised, platform dominated by an altar and its cherished scrolls—all presided over by an old, thin, white-bearded rebbe, his body clothed in a muslin prayer shawl and simple black yarmulke. Behind them, silhouetted against a badly worn cotton curtain that separated them from their menfolk, a handful of women and young girls, voices less regularly joined in chorus.

A far cry from *The Jazz Singer*, Zack thought, as he and Morrie moved to the back of the musty, windowless brownstone basement shul, looking both for a place to pray and for Morrie's father. Zack had already seen the movie three times since it came out at the end of last season. Just the chance to hear Al Jolson sing in the first "talkie" was reason enough.

But he also liked the story and always cried at the ending. Jakie Rabinowitz, spurned by his father for refusing to follow in his footsteps and become a cantor, returns home to the Lower East Side as a popular jazz singer, only to find his father on his deathbed. Jakie postpones his Broadway debut and instead sings Kol Nidre to his father's congregation while his old man dies in peace, his son returned, his dream fulfilled. Maybe. Time passes and the movie closes with Jakie back on Broadway, in blackface, singing "Mammy" before a packed house that includes his joyous, tearful mother. Baseball wasn't that far from Broadway, Zack chuckled to himself. Perhaps Morrie and his father would be as fortunate. So long as nobody dies.

Arriving a half-hour late was not a good way to start. Not that they had meant to miss meeting Jake in front of the shul before services began. But the game at the Stadium had run late. And they stayed around, with most of the large weekday crowd, to cheer the Babe who had hit his sixtieth home run in the fourth inning. By the time they got to Radio City to pick up Doris it was 5:30. Not that it mattered. When they got to the stage door, instead of Doris they found a note informing them that she had been called to an emergency rehearsal and would meet them at Morrie's house around 7:30.

———————

[Come on, sonny! Don't be so heavy-handed with the Jewish stuff. I mean *The Jazz Singer!* For Christ's sake! O.K. So you know that the movie opened on October 6, 1927. But, my shena punim, did you know that the movie ends differently from the play which preceded it? In the original version Jakie gives up Broadway and takes over for his father. Where are you heading with all this? At least we can be thankful you didn't throw in the Neil Diamond rock star version. I swear, kid, when that guy sings "America—they're all comin to America,"—that immigrant shrimp boat rock version of the American melting pot and Laurence Olivier who plays his cantor father (one of his less-convincing roles, I tell you) starts to cry in the audience, I almost puked. By the way, I know you're taking limits because this is fiction, but I didn't hit my sixtieth until later that week; it was on September 30, against Tom Zachary of the Senators—in the eighth inning, not the fourth. And just to keep the record straight for anybody reading this who doesn't know shit about baseball, it was 1927 not 1928. Which reminds me of a great joke about a broad who could never get a date because she had such an ugly face. To make a long story short, after many years of disappointment, she finally goes to a Chinese doctor to find out what's the problem. He asks her to strip, examines her from head to toe, and then asks her to bend over and put her head between her legs. After walking around her, he thinks for a moment and then exclaims in broken English: "Aha! I know why you never have date." "Why?" she asks. "Because," the doc says, "your face look zachary like your asshole!"]

———————
——

Morrie found talaysim and yarmulkes in a cardboard box behind the last bench. Handing a set to Zack, he was astonished to see his catcher knowingly kiss the tzitzit and deftly flip the prayer shawl over his newly covered head as if he had been doing it for years. Before he could say anything, Zack smiled at him, motioned to some empty spaces on the other side of the shul, in the third row from the back. "It's like learning signs, Morrie," he whispered. "Once you know how many fingers mean a curve ball, you never forget."

Morrie followed his catcher to their seats, squeezing among the knees and bodies of neighborhood men variously engaged in the proceedings at hand. Most seemed oblivious to their intrusion, barely shifting in their seats as they continued their chants. Several of them, however, grabbed at his hands, interrupting their prayers with barely audible greetings in praise of Jake's boy, their American hero.

Jake, across the basement in an aisle seat next to Max, took it all in. Anxiously, he had awaited Morrie's arrival—both angry that his boy was late yet relieved when he had not shown up on time—grateful for the temporary postponement of an evening together that filled him with uncertainty.

Max had not been so fortunate. Five minutes before it was time to go inside—as the two of them mingled with the other men and their sons, all dressed in their holiday best, Shlomo arrived.

"Well, hello, Shlomo," Jake hesitantly greeted him, even as Max turned his back.

Jake had not seen him in a while. Once in the last two months and then only from across the street—the boy in tow behind his two gonniff friends coming out of Steinberg's Delicatessen. Today he looked different—less flashy, a pentinent look on his face, even if his black, slick-backed, bear-greased hair reminded Jake of Benny Leonard—the Great Bennah, retired now, but the undisputed middleweight champion of all time. At least for Jews. More important to Jews than Einstein, the *Forward* trumpeted, when Benny retired in 1925. Tough fists for true respect, Jake remembered, Cahan had said. And his pictures. Put them in a scrapbook, Esther once told Morrie, who dutifully kept track of his hero by cutting out news photos—from his first champion fight in 1917 to that picture of him at the Roxy with Jolson. And now he was saving papers like his son. . . .

Max had no time for such thoughts. Shlomo nodded at Jake but went straight for his father. Grabbing him firmly on the forearm, he whispered into his ears words that Jake could not hear. Max said nothing. When the doors opened, Shlomo dutifully followed them in. Now father and son sat next to him, both attentive to their prayers, crowded shoulder against shoulder.

Morrie spied the trio, his father now focused on the rebbe. "My God, tonight will be very interesting," he thought, his eyes searching the room for other familiar faces.

There, sitting together a few rows behind his father were the Dux. Not that they had on their black satin jackets with the club name on them, but virtually everyone in the neighborhood, except for the oldest, most orthodox, white-bearded Russian patriarchs who still refused to accept that they now lived in a new country, knew his old high school friends by their basketball club name. It had been almost a year since Morrie had seen his old friends together. He knew they had been to the Polo Grounds for his debut and Burtie had even dropped by at the party at his house that night. But they barely had a chance to say hello amidst the crush of well-wishers who piled into the brownstone to offer their congratulations. Seeing them together now reminded Morrie how much his life had changed in so short of time.

Chilled and exhilarated by the thought, he, too, turned his attention to the service. He never liked going to shul, something he had in common with his father who never insisted that he make it part of his daily routine. Not that it was ever discussed whether or not Morrie would go to cheder or be bar mitzvahed. That was a given. But except for that, the High Holidays, and sometimes, Passover, prayer was up to him.

For Morrie it was simple. It took time away from playing ball, from stoops, streets and school yards filled with raucous, sweaty American dreams. Besides, no one ever took the time to explain what it was they were saying. Still, the chants he knew by heart. He also liked some of the stories from the Torah. And the meaning of these most holiest of days could not escape anyone who grew up on Sackman Street—this time that celebrated the end of the year-long reading of the Torah, a time of humble prayer to God for atonement, forgiveness, and renewal, not just for yourself, but for everyone—not for fathers or sons alone, but for them together, along with everyone else.

Morrie had meant to tell some of this to Zack on the train in from Manhattan. But they were so excited about the Babe's prodigious feat that he had forgotten and Zack had never asked.

"Sh'ma Yisra'el, Adonai Eloheinu, Adonai Ekhad. Br'uch shem k'vod. . . ." This most familiar and significant of all Jewish prayers, delivered from the mouth of his Giants' teammate who calmly tapped him on the shoulder to remind him to stand up and join the chorus, brought Morrie to his feet and his senses. Stuffed derma and matzo ball soup was one thing. Anyone on the road long enough— alright anyone that is besides that shmuck Hornsby—might well have stumbled into a kosher delicatessen and discovered Jewish delicacies, but this Zack would have to explain!

Max, too, demanded an explanation. He had not expected to see his son again. Not at shul, not ever again. If Essie knew this was going to happen, she had said nothing to him. Nor did he respond to Shlomo's whispered pleas of apology and forgiveness. How could he, there, in front of his friends who must have been as shocked as he was to see the dead rise up at this holiest of times? And only moments before it was time to pray? Forgive without an explanation, just because he asked? No, Max thought, as he mouthed the Shem'a, his ears filled with the still tender voice of his flesh and blood who offered the same words, his eyes fixed on the bima in prayerful attention.

————————
————

Doris paid attention, too, her ears full of clattering subway cars rumbling on metal tracks through Brooklyn streets—mostly empty now even though she was running late—abandoned long before the usual rush hour by Jewish men home early from Manhattan sweatshops and cutting rooms to mark the beginning of Rosh Hashanah.

Clad in scanty satin and spangles, high-kicking can-can legs performing intricate dance steps before Radio City whistle-hooting tourists never made Doris nervous. But here, alone, with no one in attendance, conservatively dressed in a blue cotton suit over a long-sleeve silk blouse buttoned to her neck, she felt anxious and naked. Rehearsal had been a welcomed relief—respite from what awaited her and the chance to work up a sweat, even if a nervous energy still coursed through her body.

Doris reached for the pole in front of her seat and hoisted herself up and out the door as the train's brakes brought it to a jerking, screeching halt at the Junius Street station on the IRT New Lots line. It was just turning dark as she walked down from the elevated, exiting at the back of the train onto Livonia Avenue at the corner of Sackman Steet. On any other Monday night, the candy stores, fish markets, butchers, bakeries and other shops that lined the avenue would have been full of noise and people: men on their way home from work, women picking up last minute items for dinner, children playing ring-a-levio, stick ball and Johnny-on-the-pony competing for space in streets crowded with pushcarts and automobiles, newsies selling late editions, gum and candy, each in charge of their own corner turf, thrusting and barking their wares at every passer-by—all caught up in city sounds that Doris still found novel and exotic, so sharply contrasted with her Michigan country childhood filled with summer rustling cornfields and the playful yelping of family dogs.

Tonight, however, was strangely silent, not midwestern silent, but still silent in its own way. Stores along the street were all closed. A group of men, all dressed in long black coats and fedoras each carrying a velvet sack clutched close to their chests, hurried along the sidewalk, rushing by her in earnest contemplation. Even as she thought of stopping them to ask directions, they disappeared into tree-shaded dusk, leaving her alone and deserted. Instead, Doris reached into her purse and pulled out her dog-eared New York street guide featuring separate sections on each of the five boroughs that had stood her well during her five years in the city. Opening the page she had marked in the subway, she confirmed her route—go south down Sackman Street, two blocks, past Riverdale and Newport Streets, and then on the right, three houses down, would be Morrie's house. This was not the Brooklyn she knew best—shopping at Abraham and Strauss's or a day at Coney Island. Tonight, however, promised its own excitement.

At the very moment Doris arrived at 737 Sackman Street, another group of men, less formally dressed than the one she first observed, began their own trek to the same destination—Max and Jake in the lead, followed by Morrie, Shlomo, and Zack.

It had taken more than a few minutes to leave the shul. Brief reunions with the Dux, back-slappings and mazel tovs from some of their fathers, all slowed the procession. Younger boys who knew Morrie from the school yard and the neighborhood lingered on the edges, catching bits and pieces of conversations that tingled their ears with possibility. Imagine being so close to a young man only a few years their senior, who, if luck held out, would be pitching against Babe Ruth in no more than a week! Imagine riding Pullman coaches to faraway places like Chicago and Pittsburgh, eating in fancy restaurants, playing baseball before thousands of people in ballparks large enough to hold the entire population of their neighborhood! Do you believe that Morrie saw Babe hit his sixtieth today! A few of the more bold ones who knew their baseball players from sportspages and baseball cards even drifted over to Zack who eagerly obliged their curiosity with conversation and autographs.

"God, now I know what it's like to be you, Morrie."

"Even better than I know who you are," Morrie retorted as the two men moved away from their admirers towards the corner where Jake and Max waited, along with Shlomo who stood quietly behind them.

"Where did you learn to put on a tallis and to speak Hebrew like that? What's the story?"

"In due time, Morrie, in due time. First, let me meet your father and his friends."

Before Morrie had a chance, Jake intervened. "La shom t'ov, Morrie," he greeted his son, firmly grabbing his forearm and vigorously shaking his hand. Not waiting for Morrie to reply, Jake moved on to Zack.

"So this is the famous Mr. Taylor. Welcome to Brownsville. I am very pleased to meet you. This is my friend Max Goldstein and his son Shlomo, Dodger fans, I'm afraid, but I'm sure you understand."

"No problem, Mr. Ginsberg. Happy New Year to you and thanks for inviting me to your home."

"Home, yes, we must go home," Jake replied, "Esther and Essie must be wondering what happened to us."

"And where is your other friend Morrie, this Dotty?" Max asked, eager for any chance to avoid the inevitable struggle over what he was feeling about his own son.

"That's Doris, Max. She's meeting us at the house," Morrie offered, already perplexed by his father's greeting, far warmer than he had any reason to anticipate.

"All the more reason to get going," Jake exhorted, turning the corner and heading down Sackman Street. "I want to meet this Doris."

◇

15

"SO THIS MUST BE Doris! Come in dear."

Doris stepped over the threshold directly into the Ginsberg kitchen, onto a floor still covered with newspapers, a room filled with smells totally alien from any kitchen with which she was familiar. To her left, the four-burner gas stove seemed overburdened by large cast-iron black pots, some covered, others emitting intermittent bursts of steam from under their heavy lids—all surrounded by a white porcelain surface crowded with plates of what appeared to be differently shaped dumplings. Mingled smells of overcooked meat and freshly baked bread filled her nostrils. On Doris's right a kitchen table, next to two windows open to an alleyway between brownstones caught her eye—a nothing special wooden table laden with some sort of twisted yellow-glazed bread, steamed vegetables, a chocolate cake, other foods totally unfamiliar, as well as empty platters awaiting whatever was still cooking.

Taken by the smells and sights; surprised and somewhat disappointed that Morrie had not opened the door, it took Doris a few seconds to blurt out her own response.

"It's so nice to meet you Mrs. Ginsberg, Morrie has told me a lot about you. I hope I'm not too early."

"No, you're fine, but I'm not Esther, I'm Essie Goldstein, good friend and neighbor. Call me Essie. Esther will be out in a minute. Here, let me take your jacket."

From her bedroom off the kitchen, Esther heard every word. It wasn't enough that Jake and Morrie would be home soon, and who knew in what state. Now the first girl that Morrie ever brought home had brought herself, first! Before she even had time to pick the newspapers off the floor! And a shiksa, no less! "Ach," Esther moaned, as she put on a clean, cotton flower print dress, her thoughts interrupted by the rustling of paper and by Essie's insistence that she didn't need any help cleaning up the kitchen floor.

A moment later, when she entered her domain, she found Doris and Essie laughingly pushing the last pieces of newsprint into a garbage bag under the kitchen sink. Doris looked up immediately, surprised that Mrs. Ginsberg was even smaller than Morrie had described—no more than 5 feet tall, heavy-set like he had said, her graying hair pulled back into a bun; her large, firm hands her most striking feature.

"Mrs. Ginsberg, I'm sorry if I got here a little early. I had a late rehearsal and Morrie couldn't pick me up so we could come together. He said he was going to call you."

"That's alright. He didn't call, but he has so much of this baseball to think about. Anyway you are here."

"Such a pretty girl, even if she doesn't look Jewish. So tall, thin, and blond. And such long legs. Must be from so much dancing." All this Esther thought as she slowly reached out to shake the offered hand of her son's new friend.

"Everything smells so wonderful, Mrs. Ginsberg. Please, tell me what you and Mrs. Goldstein, I mean Essie, are cooking."

"Here, start with a kreplach, darling," Essie intruded, pushing one still warm in front of Doris from the platter on the stove. "They're my specialty."

"What's in it? It looks a little bit like what the Italians call ravioli."

"I don't know from ravioli. It's just a little chopped meat, some onions, garlic, a little pepper and a bit of schmaltz stuffed into homemade dough. We'll have them later with chicken soup but they're good just like this."

"Schmaltz? I don't think I've ever heard of that before. Is it a spice or something?"

"A something," Essie laughed. "Just take a bite and see."

Although Essie's answer hardly relieved her tense stomach, Doris smiled back, tentatively took the offering from the spoon that Essie held before her, and nibbled into the still warm, moist doughy ball.

"Don't be afraid! Take a bite, it won't bite back," Essie insisted, as she watched Doris's tentative teeth do exploratory surgery on her innocent delicacy.

"Essie, leave her alone, let her eat the way she wants to," Esther retorted, embarrassed by her friend's boldness with this new person in her son's life.

"It's alright, Mrs. Ginsberg, really," Doris laughingly replied, having finally swallowed the bite of kreplach that the two women had argued about.

"Mrs. Goldstein is right. That's what my mother says, in her own way, of course. 'Stop pecking at your food like a bird, dear,' that's her line. It's a habit I picked up from my father. He always nibbled new food very carefully to make sure he liked the taste before he swallowed. Anyway, the kreplak was delicious."

Doris popped the remainder in her mouth, taking bites that would make her mother proud.

"That's kreplach, dear, not lak. Say the end like you're gargling with salt water like when you have a sore throat."

"Essie, enough already. Let her alone. Here. Why don't you go sit down at the dining room table while we finish with the food. The men should be home very soon now."

With that Esther took Doris' arm and took five steps into the rest of the railroad brownstone apartment—a long narrow room that opened on the other side of the kitchen from the bedrooms. Dominated by a table that filled it from end to end, the dining room comprised the middle of the apartment. On its other side was a small parlor with wooden bay windows that looked out onto Sackman Street.

Draped in a white, hand-made embroidered cloth and surrounded by eight high-backed, ornately carved Chippendale mahogany chairs with red velvet cushioned seats, the table was set for its full complement. Each place setting consisted of a plain white china plate, finely polished silverplate fork, knife, and spoon, and wine glass. The only other piece of furniture in this narrow room whose exterior wall contained windows that looked out onto the same alley as the kitchen window from where Jake had plucked the tomato that splat all over the Polo Grounds during Morrie's Giants debut, was a large credenza that ran the length of the room's interior wall. Its top, Doris noticed, as Esther escorted her into the room, was dominated by a pair of large brass candlesticks surrounded by framed photographs of what she took to be family.

"Really, Mrs. Ginsberg, let me help you in the kitchen. It's been a long time since I've been in one so busy and that smelled so good."

Esther shrugged her shoulders. "The water glasses are in the cupboard over the kitchen sink. I'll ask you to fill them with. . . ."

The noise of heavy footsteps coming up the stairs cut short Esther's directions and sent her waddling into the kitchen, waving her hand to Doris in apology. What was next she didn't know. But at least she knew Morrie was home.

ESSIE ALMOST FAINTED on the spot as she opened the door. The sight of her son whom she had not seen nor heard from in a year was too much even for her sturdy stock.

"You've come home mein bubela. Home!" she managed, after Max propped her up against the kitchen sink and her son patted her wrists and forehead with a damp dish towel that Esther provided.

"Yes Ma, I'm home," Shlomo softly whispered, almost as if to keep the news from his father.

Sure now that Essie was O.K., Esther stepped over her friend to embrace and kiss her most treasured possessions—Morrie first, then Jake.

Untangling himself from his mother's grip, Morrie stepped into the kitchen, smiled weakly at Doris, and with some reserve took her by the hand and introduced her to Jake as his "new friend."

"Such a pretty friend, too," Jake responded shaking her hand and passing her on to Max.

"Ah my son's catcher," Esther announced, greeting Zack as he finally made his way into the kitchen, still flush with his first encounter with Jewish prayer since he traded in his real name for a chance in the bigs.

Stumbling for position as well as for words, hands were shook, bodies shifted, in Essie's case, even lifted, before the cast moved into the dining room to begin the evening's celebration.

"And so, a happy New Year to everyone."

This Jake offered from the head of the table, his back to the kitchen, lifting his wine glass to the assembled; his enthusiasm tempered by his own ambivalence and by the crowded greetings—spoken and unspoken—that had filled an already overstuffed kitchen.

More quickly than anyone else, Zack reacted to Jake's toast. "L'chaim, Mr. Ginsberg," he responded heartily, raising from his seat between Shlomo and Max at the far end of the table.

Zack's command of language and accent stopped even Essie and Esther from their appointed tasks. The two women seated opposite each other at Jake's end of the table, had bounced to their feet on Jake's toast to begin what would be the constant shuffle of plates and bowls from kitchen to dining room. Now they hovered between the rooms as Morrie, no longer surprised at anything that came out of his friend's mouth, again demanded an explanation.

"Alright Zack, you told me in synagogue that 'in due time' you would explain to me how you know so much about Jewish things. The time is now due, nu?"

"What kind of explanation?" Esther asked.

"Ma, you should see how much he enjoys the food Jewish fans give me on the road, kisha, matzo ball soup, kasha varnishkes. . . ."

"On the road?"

"You know, when we travel to play baseball out of the city, like in Pittsburgh or Chicago. Anyway, most of the guys on the team won't even taste the stuff, but here's Zack, not only eating for three but explaining to them what goes into kisha and how schmaltz is good for their aches and pains."

"What is schmaltz, anyway?" Doris intruded.

"Schmaltz is fat from the chicken usually skimmed off the top of chicken soup after it hardens in the refrigerator. It's like Jewish crisco," Zack laughlingly explained, before anyone else had a chance to respond.

"You see what I mean!" Morrie exploded, complicating any chance Doris had to digest this unsettling news. "This goes on all the time. And tonight in shul, you seemed right at home, chanting and davening as if you've been doing it all your life. What is going on?"

"Alright Morrie, it's time to tell. The simple truth is that my real name is not Zack Taylor. Ten years ago, when I began playing baseball, a Jew didn't have a chance if he didn't change his name. So like a bunch of other guys—you know, people like Harry Kane, Broadway Smith, Phil Cooney, and Sammy Bohne, I took on a new name."

"Kane I knew about," Max interrupted, but 'Broadway Smith'? Now this is news."

"I told people I was from Alabama," Zack continued, "even took on a southern accent, which wasn't that hard for me since I was born in Florida and I learned how to change my voice from my parents who did vaudeville in the Catskills. Then you came along."

"I don't understand," Morrie said.

"Well, being with you on the road and seeing some of the rough stuff you've had to put up with from guys like Hornsby made me realize it was time to stop fooling myself. Besides look at all the free food and marriage offers you keep getting? So, in the spirit of the new year and out of my love of kreplach and that brisket I smell still simmering in the oven, I give you Philly Schwartz."

"Gevalt, the brisket!" Esther cried, breaking the attentive silence that had engulfed the table during Zack's revelation. "I would like to hear more about these 'marriage offers,' but I must take care of the main course. Come Essie. . . ."

"Please don't apologize, Mrs. Ginsberg, I'm finished anyway. And please, just call me Philly."

"Philly, that's quite a story," Max interjected, so taken by Zack's tale that he forgot for the moment his own confusion about Shlomo's presence.

"Are you sure this is Rosh Hashanah and not Purim?" Jake added, shaking his head, "Such a megillah!"

Zack caught Doris's quizzical look first. " Megillah means story and Purim. . . ."

"Alright Zack. Excuse me, I mean Philly," Morrie laughed, "enough already. So now I know why you always wait until everyone clears out of the shower before you go in."

"You see Doris . . ." Philly began to explain.

"That much about Jewish custom I know," Doris insisted.

"Oh really?" the catcher laughed, as his embarrassed battery mate coughed into his napkin.

"I mean. . . ."

"It's alright, dear," Essie interrupted. "Come. Help us in the kitchen." Which Doris did, carrying out, with Essie and Esther, the first course—plates of gefilte fish, several small bowls of horserad-ish, and on a silver platter covered with a white linen napkin, two loaves of freshly baked challah. With everything in place they took their places, awaiting Jake's prayer over the bread to begin the meal.

Engaged in his own masquerade, Shlomo, who, aside from greeting his mother, had barely spoken since leaving shul, turned to the Giants' newest Jew and broke his silence.

"I know I don't know you at all. But, let me offer you some advice."

"Please, go ahead," Philly responded.

"For the last three years, I too have been another person. . . ."

"Shlomo, this is not the place!" Max shouted angrily.

"If not here, where Pa. I came here tonight to tell you I am sorry for who I have been for the last few years and for what it has done to you and Ma. I was wrong. I admit it. I want everyone to know. That's what I mean to tell you. It's no good to hide yourself from anyone once you've made up your mind to come clean."

Before Philly could answer, Essie was at her son's side, burying his head in her breasts, comforting and suffocating in the same action.

"Max, why don't you say the prayer over the challah? Then we can begin our meal," Jake interrupted, saving his best friend from any further response.

Max accepted the honor, said the motzi and the meal commenced. One course followed another—gefilte fish, chicken soup with kreplach, then pot roast, potato kugel, tsmmis—not a sign of any green vegetable to break the pale color scheme of East European cooking—served in enormous quantities by Essie and Esther who barely sat down long enough to enjoy any of what they had prepared—all washed down by sweet holiday wine and seltzer spritzes from green-colored bottles that adorned the table.

Philly praised all that he tasted, questioning both cooks in ways that flattered their skills and impressed everyone with his knowledge of Jewish food—constant chatter and consumption that prevented any return to more pressing family matters between fathers and sons.

Somewhere between bites of brisket and kugel, Jake interrupted Philly's culinary disquisition with a question about another subject about which the Giant catcher was knowledgable.

"So Phil, how do you like your chances against the Yankees?"

"First we have to beat the Pittsburghs," this not from catcher, pitcher, Shlomo or Max but from Esther, who heard the question on the fly, back from one of her innumerable trips to the kitchen, this time returning with a platter of fried kreplach that her son's catcher had requested.

"Ma, how do you know about the Pirates?" Morrie's comment almost muffled by Essie's laughter.

"Yes, Esther dear, tell us more about this baseball," echoed Jake.

"What, Jake, do you think you're the only one who can understand such a game? You think only you read the baseball news you save in those papers?"

"What newspapers, Ma?" Morrie inquired.

"Ssh, Morrie, let your mother finish."

"Every morning since you started with the Giants, your father reads the paper and commands me to save them—at least any one that mentions your name! You should see the stack. . . ."

"Esther, this is none of anybody's business!" Jake shouted.

"Why not Jake? Why not at least let Morrie know how exciting it is for you to see his name?"

Jake waved Esther off with his hand and refilled his wine glass.

"Is this true Pa?" Morrie asked, too surprised to retort.

[That's all? No patricidal outburst? No bearing and beating of breasts? Shouldn't there be more Sturm and Drang? More tszurris and less tzismmis? Sheet, here's the place to hang out all that frustration and anger for a father Morrie loves but who shows him little love in return. What are you afraid of, the consequences? Will his worst fears be realized? Or, just as worse, will Jake, by simply not understanding, condemn his son to a purgatory of uncertainty and doubt? Or maybe, just maybe, if he takes the chance, will Jake change and become the understanding and loving father that Morrie seeks? Or maybe, just maybe, you're getting the point. After all this is the 1920s—before a comfortable middle-class affluence redefined what it was to be a "good" parent for generations twice-removed from their immigrant roots—when putting the food on the table and a roof over your family's head was proof enough of your good intentions and love, if anyone stopped to question. Not that guys like Morrie and me didn't care about what our fathers and mothers thought about us. Shit, that's a perennial question. But. . . .]

"I read the papers, I see your name. That's all."

For a moment, silence, then Esther continued, "Anyway, I read about Morrie in the *Forvetz*. Mr. Cahan tells me all I need to know. Until the Giants win two more games from the Pittsburghs, they do not get to play the Yankees, you understand?"

Even Max and Shlomo, who had found nothing amusing about their reunion, burst into laughter at Esther's remarks. "Thanks for the tip Mrs. Ginsberg," Shlomo responded. "So, Philly, when and if you do get past the Pirates, what do you think?"

"Well, 'keed,' as the Babe would say, we'll sure have our work cut out for us. We watched them today. I'm not telling you nothing you don't already know when I say that they're loaded. And not just at the plate. I mean with Ruether, Hoyt, Shocker, Moore, and Pennock, they have the best pitching staff in baseball."

"True," Doris intervened, "but how can they compete with baseball's only Jewish battery!"

Doris's quip puzzled both Morrie and Esther. While Jake quietly explained the meaning of "battery" to his wife, Morrie sought his own clarity.

"What's that supposed to mean Doris?" he barked, surprising himself with the angry tone of his voice. "Don't you think we're good enough to beat them?"

Before Doris had a chance to answer, in the spirit of a household familiar to his own where everybody else answered anybody's question even if it was not directed at them, Philly spoke up.

"Morrie, relax. Of course she does. Anything can happen in a short series. All she meant was that our news might surprise the Yanks and help our chances," spoken as if he was calming him down on the mound in the middle of the Polo Grounds with the tying run at the plate.

"That's what I'm thinking, that's what I'm thinking. All the smart money is gonna go with the Yanks but if I was still betting, I'd ride you and Morrie all the way. At least, if you make it, I'll get to see you try. You and Mr. Ginsberg too, Pa."

With that Shlomo reached into his inside jacket pocket and produced the World Series tickets that Shikey had given him only a few hours earlier. Carefully he spread them out on the table—three tickets each for the third and seventh games of the Series.

"The way I figure it," he explained, "if you get to the Series, Morrie is a cinch to pitch at the Polo Grounds in game three. If it goes seven, and McGraw plays his hunches, he'll use you again at the stadium. What do you think?"

Before either Morrie or Philly could respond, Max slammed his fist on the table, shaking the plates in front of him and turning over his wine glass—the red liquid spreading rapidly in front of him almost as fast as his face turned the same color.

"So this is how you come home! I thought you said you were through with those gonniffs! Who did you beat up to get these tickets? Ach! So much treyf!" and with those words Max reached across the table, scooped up the tickets in his right hand and flung them to the floor in disgust.

"Wait a minute Pa," Shlomo shouted back as he bent over to pick them up. "It wasn't like that. When I split I had some money coming to me. Some of the boys had an in with the ticket guy at the Stadium and got a bunch of tickets. So I just took my pay in kind. Dammit, I thought you and Mr. Ginsberg would be pleased."

"Max, please, listen to Shlomo," Essie counseled. "He meant well."

"What do you think Jake?" Max finally replied. "Do you want to go see Morrie pitch?"

"Mendelsohn won't be too happy if we miss work right in the middle of the busy season," Jake countered.

"Ach! Don't worry about him," Essie responded. "If Morrie pitches it will be another holiday—a second Jewish New Year."

Wait a minute," Morrie interrupted. "We haven't won the

pennant yet, and besides who knows when and if I'll even pitch if we do?"

"Still, if you don't mind my opinion, why not take the tickets?" Philly suggested. "As they say, it couldn't hurt."

"Yes, take the tickets Jake," Esther softly spoke.

"I don't know. Even Morrie said he may not even pitch."

"Maybe you should take the tickets, Pa," Morrie offered. "Like Philly said, 'it couldn't hurt.'"

"Take them already Jake," Max spoke up.

Before Jake could respond, Essie broke in: "Sholmo, it was nice of you to think of your father and Jake. But tell me, do you think you could also get a ticket or two for me and Esther?"

"Don't worry. If we get that far I'll give you the tickets I get. We do get tickets, don't we Philly?"

"Yes Morrie. And you can have one of mine too, Mrs. Goldstein—as partial repayment for this wonderful meal. Don't worry Doris, I'll find one for you too."

"Fine! If everyone is going to Yankee Stadium, I will go too," Jake proclaimed. "Now, what's for dessert?"

"Hold your horses," Esther came back. "The chocolate cake is coming. But first, Moey, I want to know about those marriage proposals."

SURROUNDED BY HIS own silence, the Babe sat alone in his hotel room, a half-eaten steak dinner pushed across the table, late editions of New York newspapers scattered in front of him. Slowly he
turned their pages, stopping only when he came to the sportspages
and the numerous accounts of his most prodigious feat written by
his friends.

"Well, the Babe went and did it!" Fred Lieb declared for his New
York *Post* readers. "Ten thousand fans shouted themselves hoarse
when a terrific clout from George Ruth's bat sailed into the right-
field bleachers for the big fellow's sixtieth home run. It is doubtful
if anyone in that crowd will ever live to see another player hit his
sixtieth home run in a 154 game season."

Ruth nodded in agreement and smiled at Freddy's description
of the crowd's eruption when he took Tom Zachary's pitch deep into
the right-field bleachers. The other papers followed suit, requiring

less of the Babe's attention as he quickly confirmed their affirmation of his greatness.

Only one other column really caught his attention—a poem by John Kieran. Ruth read it carefully, his right index finger moving slowly under each word to make sure he didn't miss a thing.

You may sing your song of the good old days till the phantom cows
    come home;
You may dig up glorious deeds of yore from many a dusty tome;
You may rise to tell of Rube Waddell and the way he bussed them
    through,
And top it all with the great fast ball that Rusie's rooters knew.
You may rant of Brouthers, Keefe, and Ward and half a dozen more;
You may quote by rote from the record book in a way that I deplore;
You may rave, I say, till the break of day, but the truth remains the
    truth:
From "One Ole Cat" to the last "At Bat," was there ever a guy like
    Ruth?

He can start and go, he can catch and throw, he can field with the
    very best.
He's the Prince of Ash and the King of Crash, and that's not an idle
    jest.
He can hit the ball o'er the garden wall, high up and far away.

Beyond the uttermost picket lines where the fleet-foot fielders stray.

He's the Bogey Man of the pitching clan and he clubs 'em soon and
late;

He has manned his guns and hit home runs from here to the Golden
Gate;

With vim and verve he has walloped the curve from Texas to Duluth,

Which is no small task, and I beg to ask: Was there ever a guy like
Ruth?

———————
————

You may rise and sing till the rafters ring that sad and sorrowful
strain;

"They strive and fail—it's the old, old tale; they never come back
again."

Yes, it's in the dope, when they hit the slope they're off for the shad-
owed vale,

But the great big Bam with the circuit slam came back on the uphill
trail;

Came back with cheers from the drifted years where the best of them
go down;

Came back once more with a record score to wear a brighter crown.

My voice may be loud above the crowd and my words just a bit un-
couth,

But I'll stand and shout till the last man's out: There was never a guy
like Ruth.

———————
————

"Never a guy like Ruth! Never a guy like Ruth! Never a guy like Ruth! Ruth! Ruth! Ruth!" The poem's sweet refrain rattled around in his head, pounding outward on his temples, threatening to explode and shatter the greatest baseball player the game had ever seen.

Only hours before he had been bouncing around the Yankee clubhouse like a little boy, exuberant in his triumph, back-slapped and back-slapping, stark naked before Kieran and the other press who crowded around his cubicle, waiting on his every word.

"Hey, do you think you'll break sixty next year?"

"I don't know and I don't care, but if I don't, I know who will. Wait till that bozo Gehrig starts wading into them again and they'll forget that a guy named Ruth ever lived."

"C'mon Jidge," Artie Mann of the *Evening World* retorted. "If the world forgets that a guy named Ruth lived, it will be due to universal amnesia!"

Babe had joined in the approving laughter that followed, but the thought stayed with him in other ways—made him beg off Benny and Dutch's entreaties to drive out to the Blossom Heath where legions of his closest friends and admirers awaited his triumphal presence and sent him instead to his hotel suite.

Ruth crumpled Kieran's column into a tight ball and hurled it against the hotel room wall.

"Amnesia! I wish I still had it," he muttered. "No such luck! Not since I ran into that Greenstein kid. Fathers, sons, Baltimore orphan homes, that's all that I think about! Me, the Sultan of Swat, the man who makes Casey look like a minor leaguer! Shit, I hope that kid had better luck with his poem and his father than I'm having with mine."

[And I suppose now you'll have me pick up the phone, call George, Sr. in Baltimore and invite him to the World Series? Don't even think it. I appreciate the sensitivity and psychological angst you're bringing out in me. I mean not one of the books written about me even begins to tap the depths of my psyche and soul. At best, in the hands of an occasional skilled historian, I become a hero of excess and curious nostalgia, well-suited to the 1920s. But the others don't even come close to capturing my complexity. So stay with it. Just don't get too sloppy or contrived. Shit! I hate it when that happens.]

———————

———

"Not that I've been in touch with him for a while. Let's see. I saw him in Washington in May or June when we came through to play the Senators. And then I sent him a check in July to help him pay off his mortgage on the saloon."

Babe got up, retrieved the newsprint that contained Kieran's poem, and smoothed it out on the desktop that doubled as his dining room table.

Fumbling through the desk drawer, he took out an envelope, brown-embossed with the Alamac's name and picture, ripped off the part of the page that contained the poem, folded it up, and stuffed it in the envelope and addressed it his father. On a piece of hotel stationery, he penned a brief accompanying note:

"Thought you might like to see this. Your son, George."

With that, Babe headed out the door, envelope in hand. It wasn't too late to catch a cab for Long Island.

◇

18

DRESSED IN HIS GAME-DAY suit of white linen, John McGraw leaned back in his swivel chair, propped his feet up on the corner of his desk that looked out into the Giants' clubhouse and puffed serenely on his second panatela of the morning. Reading the pages of the morning *News*, he found what he already knew. It was simple. The Pirates had folded in St. Louis, dropping their last regular season game and three out of four to the Cardinals. In the meantime his boys had split with the Cubs, Ginsberg winning on Wednesday and Benton, his ace in the hole, shelled yesterday. Now it was up to Hubbell to carry the load. If the Giants won, the pennant was theirs; if they lost, Pittsburgh backed into the World Series.

Some things made Mac nervous—too much money bet on the wrong horse; that tightening sensation that grabbed his chest, especially after he ate or drank too much—but not baseball. Pencilling in the lefthander's name in the ninth spot on his line-up card, he relished the moment. Sure, to be thirty again would be better.

Setting up shop at third base, sifting the infield dirt through his fingers, turning the double play; taking his turn at the plate—that's when he had been happiest. But even dressed in suit and tie, carrying the roster out to home plate, the thrill of the grass beneath his feet still filled him with excitement. Today, especially.

Like Ginsberg, he had brought Hubbell along slowly. Four years older than his Jewish rookie, Carl arrived in New York in June. After a slow start, the lefthander from Carthage, Missouri had come into his own, a winner in his last four starts with two shutouts to his credit. "My meal ticket," Taylor jokingly called him, after Hubbell set down Philadelphia in order. McGraw remembered that as he placed the card in his inside jacket pocket, hopeful that there was at least one more blue plate special in the young lefthander's arm.

The Cubs were no Sunday picnic, even though the best they could finish was fourth. Yesterday's thrashing proved they still had some fight left. And guys like Hack Wilson, with their own numbers on the line, were not about to lay down just because the pennant was out of reach. Not that McGraw needed reminding, but the Cubbie's squat center-fielder had led the barrage against Benton. "Baby Ruth Jostles the Jints," the *News* proclaimed—Hack's thirtieth home run, a towering three-run blast that flew into the right-field upper deck, earned him the sobriquet and tied him with St. Louis's Sunny Jim Bottomley for the National League lead.

Nothing Wilson did surprised McGraw. After all, as he reminded Jim Tierney, the club's secretary, that very morning, he had brought Hack to the Giants in 1923 and nurtured him for three seasons while he struggled at the plate.

"Fuck it, Jim, if you hadn't screwed up and left the kid's name off the club's roster for the 1926 season, the Cubs never could have picked him up and we'd all be here with hangovers from last night's celebration."

"No doubt, you're right, Skip," Tierney replied, "but we'll get 'em today. You can bet on it."

"I already did, boy, I already did. Arnold and I had dinner last night. He convinced me that the odds were right."

McGraw's other favorite Jew already was in his box seat behind the Giants' dugout. Arnold Rothstein was in a jovial mood. Dressed for a night at the opera rather than a day at the ballpark, his black wool topcoat opened to let in the warmth of a mid-afternoon September sun, he nodded to the Tammany crew in the adjoining boxes and to the businessmen with their out-of-town clients in tow who pointed him out from a distance.

Although his most productive work insisted upon private negotiations and secret deals, he welcomed and encouraged public moments of recognition. Only that morning he reread with pleasure the letter Scott Fitzgerald had written to him last year when he had sent him a copy of his new novel. "See page 88," it concluded, "You are my Meyer Wolfsheim."

"Meyer Wolfsheim, to a tee," thought Arnold, recalling from memory how his writer friend immortalized him. Nick Carraway's lunch companion, the man who could "play with the faith of fifty million people—with the singlemindedness of a burglar blowing a safe" and get away with it—the man who "just saw the opportunity" and "fixed the World Series." "Why isn't he in jail?" Carraway asks. "They can't get him, old sport," Gatsby replies, "He's a smart man."

The King of Gamblers, the Big Bank Roll, always kept his own hands clean. Monk Eastman, his childhood mentor and strong arm, and Abe Attell, "the Little Hebrew," still as tough at 44 as when he reigned as boxing's featherweight champion, took care of the dirty work—shaking down landlords, threatening jockeys and horse trainers, collecting the money, laying off the bets—while Arnold, slight and small like Attell but tough in his own way, wined and dined New York's politicos and big spenders at his New York mansion and his Saratoga Springs gambling establishment, always on the look for an edge or an opening to enhance his fortune.

"What a day Davey," Rothstein exulted, uncharacteristically slapping his diminutive companion on the back as the two men found their seats after paying their respects to the Stars and Stripes. A smiling David Weiss nodded agreeably.

It was good to be outside in the fresh air. Sometimes, before his evening shift at the Blossom Heath, in warm weather, after the tables had been set and the reservation cards placed, David, dressed in his tuxedo and patent leather shoes, strolled the inn's grounds, catching a few minutes of sunshine. But this was different.

The expectation of several hours bathed in late-afternoon September sun surrounded by fellow partisans of his favorite baseball team, all there to cheer the Giants on to victory, transformed the usually taciturn maître d' into a veritable cheerleader.

Not that his boys needed much help. Hubbell handcuffed Hartnett and Wilson at every turn with inside brush-back fast balls, followed by an unsettling array of curve balls that seemed to fall off the plate. And Davey was there with every pitch and every play— "Atta boy Carl," "Nice stop Rajah," "Play closer to the line Bill,"—a

relentless litany of encouragement and applause, full of his knowledge and love of the game.

By the seventh inning it was all over. Even allowing for a solo
blast by Hack Wilson in the top of the fourth, the Giants were up 8
to 1 and Hubbell showed no signs of tiring.

"I think it's safe for me to leave Arnold," Weiss joked with his
baseball companion, as he buttoned up his topcoat. "Will I see you
at the club later?"

"If not tonight, sometime in the next few days."

"Aren't you going to wait for the end and go into the clubhouse?"

"I wish I could Arnold, but I must get back. No doubt I'll celebrate with them at the inn tonight. Give my best to McGraw."

"I will Davey, I will. And take care of yourself."

19

BY THE TIME ARNOLD directed his driver to take him home to his Park Avenue apartment and before Davey Weiss was halfway back to the Blossom Heath, McGraw and his Giants escaped the gauntlet of delirious rooters that mobbed them on the field and made it to their clubhouse to celebrate their first pennant since 1924.

"Johnny, my boy! I knew we would do it," shouted Horace Stoneham, bear-hugging McGraw—his voice barely heard above the din brought forth by twenty-five men in various array of nakedness, slapping towels, popping champagne, swilling, spitting, splashing alcohol contraband everywhere—crowded by reporters and photographers eager to grab the next headline.

And everybody had a story. An angle on "when did you feel you were going to cop the flag?" and "what was the turning point in the season?" The hit, error, catch, inning, pitch, play, player, moment that made it happen. As if one instant or one player could single-handedly account for it all.

"What about it Morrie? The Giants were five games out in third place when you came up. Weren't you the difference? After all, you're 5 and 1 since you joined the club," Mike McConnell hawked, crowding around the young pitcher, still in undershirt and uniform pants, squeezing him against his green, metal locker bearing the white tape with his name on it that had greeted him only a few weeks ago that day when he had traveled from Brownsville to the Polo Grounds, his father's taunts about McConnell's column ringing in his ears.

"Go easy, Mikey! Enjoy yourself, have some of the bubbly," Philly intervened with his best imitation of an Irish brogue—his naked, hairy, barrel-chested torso wrapped only by a white towel, towering over the little Irish reporter as he dribbled half a bottle of bootleg over McConnell's head.

"Don't you know," Hornsby laughed, "Morrie here is the circumsized answer to McGraw's prayer!"

"No fuck head, I am," bellowed Schwartz, wheeling on the tormentor even as he whipped off his towel to reveal a neatly trimmed, erect Jewish cock to all present. "And if I hear any more crap from your mouth, Morrie and I will kick the shit out of you. Are we clear about that?"

"Hey, I was only joking with the kid," bullied-back, Hornsby retreated from center-stage, clearly heard now in a silently still clubhouse transfixed on the newly discovered member of the Giants' Jewish battery.

"Why, I'll be a son of a bitch," squeaked McConnell. "What the fuck is going on here?"

Morrie, himself ready to unload on the Jolly Rajah before Philly intervened, responded: "Mr. McConnell, I give you Philly Schwartz, the best Jewish catcher in the major leagues."

"That's Philly, as in Brotherly Love," Schwartz added, decorously replacing his towel around his waist before bowing formally to the champagne-soaked, sweated assemblage of reporters, photographers and ballplayers.

"Taylor, in my office, now! You too Ginsberg. All reporters, out of here. We'll have a statement later. Everyone else, get dressed and be back here tomorrow at noon for practice!"

McGraw's bark shattered the air with authority, sending Giants to their lockers and grumbling newsmen to the door, stumbling over each other out of the locker room on the way to call in stories.

"I'm coming, skip, but it's not Taylor, it's Schwartz with a Z."

20

AN UNUSUAL NIGHT at the Blossom Heath, at least on a night when the Babe was on view. Center stage belonged to the New York Giants, or at least that substantial handful who arrived buoyant from the Polo Grounds, fresh from unfurling Jewish pendants and baseball pennants.

By the time Morrie and Philly arrived, Hornsby, Terry, Ott, Hubbell and the rest of the crew were so deep into celebration and revelry that none of them noticed the arrival of their Jewish teammates.

A few shots of bootleg had quickly taken away the Rajah's clubhouse embarrassment, restoring him, at least for the moment, to his position as Giant leader and toastmaster—on his feet, gladhanding all who came over to congratulate his boys, ask for autographs or treat them to another round.

Even the Babe, on his way back from his usual stint at the bandstand, stopped by to pay his respects. But only for a moment, on the lookout, even as he slapped Hornsby on the back and shook hands all around, for Davey Weiss, the man whose counsel he sought on pressing business.

Surprised and taken by Babe's request, Davey had assured him, as he came in the door, that once the usual rush had subsided he'd be over. But it was almost 10, saxophone played, crowd otherwise engaged, and the Babe growing restless with no Weiss in sight; only other Jews, Giant Jews sitting on the other side of the room at their own table, set apart from their teammates and awaiting their own meeting with the master of the house.

But the master was otherwise engaged, shut off from the buzz, band, and banter less by the thin walls of his small office crushed backstage between the bandstand and the kitchen, than by the persistent demands of Shikey Friedman and Izzy Cohen who carefully laid out their threats and demands.

"Look, Mr. Weiss, it's very simple. Guilt by association. Either you come up with the cash or it's 1919 all over again, but this time everyone knows who you are."

"But Mr. Friedman, even if I admitted to your accusations and chose to protect myself, I am afraid I could not come up with your request for $40,000. What do you imagine a man of my position earns in a year?"

"A man in my position . . ." Izzy exploded. Bolting off the edge of the desk, his knuckles cracking and crackling to be put to purpose, he grabbed Weiss out of his chair by his shirt and flung him up against the wall separating the office and the kitchen.

"Look, we know you own half this place and we know who your friends are. Either you get us the money by Tuesday morning or you're dead meat. One way or another, maybe both," Izzy sneered.

"Easy Izzy, I'm sure Mr. Weiss understands our position. Please, let go of him." This said, Friedman stood up from the desk chair in which he had been patiently sitting, pulled lightly at his shirt cuffs so that the same quarter-inch of white showed beyond the end of his suit-jacket sleeves, and prepared to leave.

"We'll be back on Tuesday morning at 10. Please don't disappoint us. And please, for your own saftey, do not breathe a word of this moment to anyone. Come on Izzy, we must be going."

Reluctantly Cohen dropped Weiss off the wall, roughly straightened out the man's ruffled ruffled shirt, tweeked his bow tie, and turned and left without another word, preceding Friedman out the door down the corridor beside the bandstand, past the bathrooms, out into the ballroom, through the crowds, and into the evening's blackness.

"My God, they're all over the place," Babe muttered to himself, as they walked by his table, so deep in their own conversation that they paid no attention to New York's most recognizable citizen.

———————
——

[New York! Do you think my fame stopped at the Hudson River? For Chrissakes, by 1928 I was earning $70,000 a year; more than the President of the United States! Even then sportswriters lauded me as the man who turned the game of baseball around—made it a power game, made people forget about the Black Sox Scandal. I mean everyone knew me. My ticker-tape parade down Wall Street after we won the '27 series was even bigger than Lindy's. Men spent more time wondering about how many women I laid in a week than they fucked in a year! Shit, I was everywhere, I mean everywhere! You couldn't pick up a paper without seeing my mug. I was THE NEWS.]

———————

———

"I'll be back in a few minutes," Babe informed Dutch Ruether, who, along with Benny Bengough, had accompanied him to the club.

"Take a piss for me too, Jidge."

"Sure thing, Dutch." But the Babe—fresh from his sixtieth homer, fresh from poetic public paeans of his unique talents, already acknowledged as the greatest and most important player of the day—had other pressures on his mind as he made his way through the maze of tables and bodies, past the bathrooms, back to Weiss's office and the reason for his visit.

Not that he had carefully thought out what he would say to David Weiss—a man he had known almost from the day he arrived in New York in 1920 when someone, he couldn't remember who anymore, had taken him out to the Blossom Heath for the first time. Their conversations had been brief snatches rather than extended colloquies—the press of Weiss's duties and the occasion of Ruth's visits dictated that—mostly about the weather, the game, or the evening at hand. But intuitively, Babe understood that this man—always reserved, polite, and dignified—listened well and genuinely seemed to care about him; not as some larger than life baseball icon but as a person; someone who might keep his confidences, even if just for the opportunity to unload his troubled mind. And he sensed he was Jewish, whatever that meant—some mysterious identification that went beyond circumsized cocks, hooked noses, and wiry hair, that might help the Babe understand what Morrie Ginsberg had somehow wrought.

Unaccustomed to waiting for anyone or anything, and with the door to the office half-open, Babe knocked as he entered, only to find the maître d' prone on a settee, shirt opened at the collar and a wet towel covering his forehead.

"What's the matter Davey, my music too much for you?"

Startled by Babe's entrance, embarrassed by this witness to his own disarray, Weiss pulled back from his own thoughts and confronted his latest visitor.

"It's customary, even for you, Mr. Ruth, to knock before entering!"

"Gee, I'm sorry Mr. Weiss," Ruth sneered, "I didn't think it was any big deal." But almost as the words were out of his mouth and before Weiss had a chance to retort, the Babe's tone softened.

"Look, we said we'd talk and I just thought that maybe you forgot and well, I really have a lot on my mind and I thought you might be able to help me understand some of it as it involves, well, you see, it's about people like. . . ."

"Please, sit down Babe. And pardon my gruffness. It has been a difficult evening tonight and I just hoped to catch a brief respite before returning to the floor. Nothing more. Now, please, what is it exactly that you wanted to talk about? What PEOPLE are you talking about?"

"Now don't get me wrong. I don't mean no offense by saying this, but I'm talking about Jews. They're everywhere, Mr. Weiss."

"I don't think I'm following you very well here."

"You're right, Davey. I'm getting ahead of myself. Slow down Babe, start at the beginning," words that came as the Sultan of Swat ended his agitated pacing and settled in on the corner of Weiss's desk.

"Look, it all started about a month ago, right here. Remember when Paul introduced that new Giant pitcher, Greenbaum."

"You mean Ginsberg?"

"Yeah, that's it. Well, and don't ask me why, but ever since that night, not all the time, you know, but I've been thinking about that kid and how I helped him out with Hornsby. . . ."

"That was a nice thing you did that night but I don't really understand. . . ."

"I know Davey, I know. Well, from that night on, I also started thinking a lot about my father, about Baltimore, about the orphanage, about all kinds of shit that never crosses my mind and, although I don't understand it, nine times out of ten when I do, somehow, whether in the paper or just out of the blue, that kid comes into my mind. And tonight! I went over to the Polo Grounds to congratulate the boys, but I never got inside because it was Jew night at Coogan's Bluff!"

"Yes, I heard the news."

"And now both Hebs are sitting out there by themselves!"

"But I'm not sure why you think the fact that Morrie Ginsberg is Jewish or that your meeting him has anything to do with what comes into your mind."

"Me neither. Not exactly . . . except he was so nervous out there on the bandstand. And he's been getting so much attention, like I always get. . . . And then, last night, I went over to Radio City to catch the show and try to pick up a dancer dame I met once before. It was one thing for her to give me the cold shoulder. But she told me that she had no interest in me because she was already seeing another ballplayer. Who, I ask. Yeah, you guessed it. This Ginsberg guy."

"What a remarkable coincidence!"

"Coincidence? It's unreal. And every time he pops up, my pop comes up to me. What's going on? Does he think of his own father every time he thinks of me?"

"His father? Why? How do you know he even has one? Or that he thinks of you?"

"Everyone has a father, Mr. Weiss, even if he's dead, and every one who plays baseball thinks of me."

"But why think of your father when you think of Ginsberg? Why think of fathers at all?"

"Jesus, Davey, that's what I'm trying to figure out!"

"Perhaps you're trying too hard. Look, I have few words of wisdom to offer you. All I know is that each of us, in his own way, seeks a path in life that allows them to get along, to survive, and if fortunate enough, to enjoy what life has to offer in ways that do not do damage to others. Sometimes it's a fine line. Sometimes we botch it badly. And every once in a while, sometimes too often, we get caught up short, wondering why we do or feel what we do. Why, sometimes it seems like Purgatory!"

"Purgatory?" Babe asked. "You mean what you take when you can't take a shit?"

"No Babe, that's not quite what I meant. Look, we all handle those moments differently and different moments differently. And that includes thinking about things—about fathers even—that you haven't thought about in a long time. It's just a way of helping yourself understand something that's on your mind, even if you're not aware of it."

"But why would my father be on my mind now? I mean, shit, I just hit sixty home runs. Even I may never do better than that!"

"Does your father know?"

"Anyone whose anybody knows that!"

"But did he tell you he knows?"

"Well, I haven't heard from him, if that's what you mean."

"And he from you?"

"Probably by tomorrow. I sent him a copy of Kieran's poem. Figured he wouldn't get that in Baltimore."

Weiss smiled. He was now sitting up, so absorbed with the give and take that his own troubles momentarily removed themselves from his consciousness. Instead he remembered similar exchanges on a different subject with his own father a long time ago at the kitchen table in the apartment on Maxwell Street—in Hebrew, over Talmud—mysterious texts yearning for interpretation and understanding explored by the rabbi and his son.

"What's the smile for?"

"All this talk of fathers and sons made me think of my own father, that's all. A pleasant memory of a time when we were together, sharing something once important to both of us."

"Oh."

"Oh? And so?" like his father, he asked, "Does this suggest anything to you?"

"You see, it's happening to you. Start with that Ginsberg and you end up with your father."

"Is that so terrible, Babe?"

"No, I guess not. I mean I don't know . . . maybe my memories are not as pleasant as yours."

"Is this what is troubling you? Nothing to remember fondly, nothing to share with your father at a moment when you think that everyone wants to share your glory with you?"

Babe listened intently, searching for the insight that might settle his confusion—so intently that he didn't notice Morrie and Philly, who now appeared at Weiss's open office door.

"Think about it. In the meantime say hello to Mr. Ginsberg and Mr. Schwartz, is it?"

Actually reverse order would have been more appropriate. Even in the clubhouse, when Philly proposed a visit to Long Island to see Weiss, Morrie had been reluctant. He barely knew the man and had no interest in running into Hornsby again. But Philly insisted and his exuberance carried Morrie along.

"I hope we're not interrupting anything, Babe, but we just came by to say hello to Mr. Weiss."

Turning to Morrie, who stood behind him, his face barely visible behind the door frame filled with his battery mate's body, Philly added, "You've already met my pitcher."

"Yeah, hello kid," the Babe muttered, uncomfortably confronting the man who had become the symbol of his own discomfort.

"Well, congratulations to you both on winning the pennant, and to you Mr. Schwartz for letting the cat out of the bag, so to speak."

"Thanks Davey. I wish you could have seen it. You should have seen the look on Hornsby's face. Not that I had planned to announce anything, and certainly not the way it happened, but the jerk made one too many remarks about Jews, so I let him have it."

"And you Mr. Ginsberg, what do you think about the news?"

"Please, just call me Morrie, Mr. Weiss. Me, I already knew. I've been wondering about him almost from the day I joined the club. Zack, I mean Philly, told me the whole story when he came over to my father's house for Rosh Hashanah."

"Rash Heshena? Sounds like some kind of disease you pick up in the wrong places. What the hell is that?"

"Well, you see Babe, in the Jewish religion. . . ."

"Not now, Philly," Morrie intruded. "Enough Jewish history lessons. Look, we said hello. Let's go. We already interrupted Mr. Weiss and Mr. Ruth long enough."

"That's O.K. kid, I figured it had something to do with that. Anyways, I was just leaving," Babe admitted, wondering as he spoke how such a little shrimp of a guy, shy to boot, could appeal to any woman more than himself.

"It's alright Morrie. In fact we were just talking about you when you came in. Isn't there something you wanted to ask him Babe?"

"Yeah, sure kid," Babe stuttered, surprised by Weiss's candor, passing on the mention of Morrie's father, not yet in position to frame his inquiry but much closer than he had been before this evening at the inn.

"What day will you be on the mound?"

"Probably Saturday, the third game, at the Stadium."

"Well, just put 'em where I like him, anywheres near the plate will do," Babe commanded, slapping the young pitcher on the back as he went out the door. "See you, Davey. And thanks for the help. I'll think about what you said."

"It's none of my business, but what kind of help did you give the Babe?" Philly asked after the three watched baseball's greatest player disappear into the main ballroom.

"You are right my fine Jewish friend. It is none of your business."

"Come on Philly, we've taken up enough of Mr. Weiss's time. It's time to head back to the city. So long Mr. Weiss."

"Yeah, good bye Davey, and thanks for your help."

"What an evening it has been," Thought Weiss, as he closed the door behind his last visitors and prepared himself for his return to the floor. "A good thing, too, that tomorrow is my day off. I will have to see Arnold. He will know what to do."

◇

WILLIAM JENNINGS BRYAN in a blue-and-white-striped bathing suit—pants tight to the hips, a shirt top buttoned halfway to the neck—accentuating the rotund and sagging physique of the aging, hair-thinned firebrand—buried not on a cross of gold but buoyed by a rubber raft afloat in a swimming pool, a lemonade held high in his right hand, strawberried and strawed, needing no protection from a warm Florida sun, connected by left arm extended to the heavens—one that promised investors relaxation, ease, enjoyment, and above all, a good return on their dollar. *OR* John McGraw, Baseball Man, feet planted firm on home plate, cap on straight, bat over his left shoulder in military parade, front and center in his New York Giants uniform, his left arm, too, extended skyward—his, to the pennants over Pennant Park, with its own promise of Florida retirement and new prosperity for those with the good sense and the capital to invest in a sure thing.

Arnold Rothstein held both lithographs, one in each hand, weighed them for a moment more, and then tossed the Bryan print into his wastebasket. The old man had done well in Coral Gables, he smiled, helping to jack up land prices from the mere $800 an acre that had been Rothstein's outlay in 1921 to well over $10,000 a shot by 1925. But Bryan died that year—victim of broken heart and fundamentalist faith, lost in a struggle to the death with Clarence Darrow over Charles Darwin that he was unable to survive. Besides, Rothstein mused, the pitch in Sarasota was baseball—retire to the winter home of the New York Giants, play golf with John McGraw on the rolling greens of Pennant Park's own course, situated smack in the middle of a new tract of superior homes guaranteed to give pleasure and relaxation by none other than the famous baseball player and manager himself!

"What do you think, Davey, will Mac be pleased?" he asked his companion of yesterday's ballpark revelry who sat patiently on the other side of his desk while Rothstein made his decision.

"It is very nice Arnold. A good likeness too. I'm sure that he will approve. But now, tell me what must we do about the matter I discussed with you on the phone last night."

"The money, itself, is not a problem, David. Just a matter of taking from there and putting some here. But why now? I ask myself, aside from the obvious leverage these scum tried to use with you. What else is going on? Alone, they are nothing! Gone in a minute!" he snapped his fingers for emphasis. "But what if. . . ." Rothstein leaned back in his leather chair, puffing gently on his cigar.

"Good questions all, but there is a certain immediacy here that. . . ."

"Don't worry, David. All you will need is in here," Rothstein offered, reaching beside him for a brown leather satchel, bulged to its capacity, which he handed to Weiss. "We will give them what they ask for but we will watch it all, just the same."

———————

Across town in the darkened vom of the Music Hall, Morrie watched too—a morning brush up of chorus-line routines punctuated by high leg kicks and head turns, precisely patterned and performed by twenty-five Rockettes—each much different in appearance and outfit in rehearsal clothes than they would be for their costumed evening performance.

"Much tougher than batting practice," Morrie surprised Doris as she came off into the wings. Before she could respond, Morrie pulled her aside and continued:

"You were right about the other night. I didn't mean to ignore you in front of my parents. It wasn't on purpose. The whole evening was just so strange that I. . . ."

Doris interrupted him with a kiss. "It's alright Morrie. There was so much going on that night—Shlomo's confession, the food. My nervousness, the food. Your nervousness, the food. Zack's surprise, the food. . . .

"Your accent still stinks but your timing is getting better. By the way, it's now officially Philly Schwartz. He announced it to the world after we won the pennant."

"I read about it in the papers. Both, I mean. I should have called to congratulate you. But I was still angry. Even so, I have proof of my real feelings. How many girls, do you think, would turn down a date with the Sultan of Swat?"

"Ruth asked you out?" Morrie blurted incredulously.

"Why so surprised? Am I lacking in some way, I mean. . . ."

"No, Doris, I didn't mean to suggest that . . . well . . . ," Morrie fumbled, embarrassed to admit that he was thinking more of himself as equal to the Babe than anything else.

"Anyway I had met him once before. The night after I saw you he just came by, unannounced."

"What did you say to him?"

"I told him I was already going out with a famous baseball player."

Morrie blushed. "What did he say?"

"It was strange. At first, he wouldn't take no for an answer. He just kept kidding, asking, almost cute, in his own way. But when I mentioned your name, he turned sour. 'It figures,' he mumbled, and then he just walked off."

"Funny, I met him with Philly by chance at the Blossom Heath the next night but he didn't say a word. He just asked me to give him a good pitch to hit at next week. Speaking of which, I've got to get going."

"Come by tonight after my last show."

"I will. There's still a lot to talk about."

———————

For the first time in several weeks, the Babe awoke rested from uninterrupted sleep, a dream lingering on the surface that he rehearsed several times as he lay in the quiet of his room. He and his father at a restaurant, not any beanery—an elegantly draped room, tuxedoed waiters, fine crystal—a familiar-looking room but one that he couldn't identify. The two of them are enjoying wonderfully rich Havana cigars as just conclusion to an exquisite meal. The check arrives and his father pays the bill. Babe doesn't protest. Instead, he leaves the tip, a very generous amount, on the table. The father nods in approval and the two walk off together, arms around each other.

"Where the hell was that—the Inn, Delmonico's, the Stork Club?" Babe wondered. "Shit, I'll take him to all three when he is in town, although I'll pick up the tab."

Smiling, the dream still fresh in his mind, he picked up the house phone and called room service to order up his breakfast, making the additional request that they check with the switch board to see if there were any messages from one George Herman Ruth, Sr. from Baltimore, Maryland, whom he had telegrammed the previous evening.

———————————

Jake and Max, side by side, at the window of Mendelsohn's, their constant conversation monitored by the demanding hum of Singer sewing machines—the clicking sounds as their feet touched the pedals sending the flybelt whirring around—their hands deftly moving the cloth beneath their fingers through the stitching box.

"What time will Shlomo pick us up on Saturday?"

"Jake, this is at least the fifth time you have asked me that question since yesterday. I told you. He said 10 o'clock in the morning."

"The morning I knew. So, have you settled with him?"

"A curious question coming from a man who only a few weeks ago thought his son was a bum for spending his time playing children's games. What happened?"

"I didn't ask you for a question, only for a yes or no," Jake persisted, reaching over for still another pair of trousers in need of cuffs.

"Jake. . . ."

"Did I ever tell you how when I was little, when we first moved to Brownsville, I used to play a game called 'one o' cat'"?

"No."

"It was like baseball, a little. It only took three kids, something for a ball and a bat. And sometimes I would go over to where the Dodgers used to play, over on Eastern Parkway near Pitkin, and watch through the crack in the outfield fence. Especially I liked to watch the pitchers, so graceful and strong. In control of the game."

"So what does this have to do with my question?" Max insisted.

"None of this I ever told to Morrie," Jake responded, his fingers deftly moving the next pair of pants in place as he talked.

"So?" Max persisted.

"So, if everybody else wants to see Morrie play baseball, why shouldn't I go too? Besides, he makes more throwing a baseball than I will ever stitching a hem. And look how much fresh air he gets! What a wonderful country this America is."

"Such wonderful I could live without. Your son the baseball player and my son the gangster! Only in America!"

"So Max. You never answered my question," Jake reminded his friend.

But Max refused to answer, head down, hands buried in still another pair of blue serge pants relentlessly awaiting his finisher's touch.

--

"Don't worry, Just take your father and Jake to the game and enjoy yourself. It will just be the three of you, right?"

"Yeah, I convinced Morrie to hold off on tickets for our mothers. Said it would be better for me if this was just a father and son thing. They were a little disappointed but. . . ."

"Good! And don't worry about what will happen. Tomorrow we bet on the Giants. They're at home and due for a win. If all goes well, next Thursday we'll cash it all in."

"Don't worry, Fats," Shikey continued, aware of his sidekick's uncertainty. "We'll just keep them incognito so to speak, until we collect our due. Then we'll let them go. Believe me, they're not going to go running to the police."

"Who gives a shit?" Izzy interrupted. "Just be sure on Thursday, you are where you are supposed to be by 11:30. We'll take over from there."

"Take it easy, Izzy, That's why tomorrow is a nice dry run. This is not an easy thing for him to do. But in the end, he will enjoy it the most, eh? What do you say, Fats?"

"Yeah, sure Shikey," Max's boy responded, although his words carried more conviction than he felt in his heart.

———————

Essie and Esther, side by side, walked down Pitkin Avenue past Mendelsohn's and the conversations of their husbands, on their way to the fruit store, the grocery, the bakery, and the butcher—cotton cloth house dresses under their woolen buttoned sweaters, empty baskets in their hands and determination in their voices.

"I don't care what Morrie says. Fathers and sons are important but why should we not see this World Series?"

"You're right. But Cahan says in the paper that there are no tickets for sale for any games so don't bother to go on Saturday when Morrie pitches."

"Yes, but Cahan doesn't know my son's catcher. He said he would get us tickets."

"Good. Then it's settled. We will call this Philly and tell him to get us tickets. Do you have his number?"

"Why should I have his number? But I know who does. Do you think they have a telephone at Radio City?"

SHLOMO STEERED THE Packard down Sackman Street toward
Pitkin Avenue, past Mendelsohn's and the storefronts that he knew
so well, his father alongside and Jake, more comfortably dressed
than his last visit to the Polo Grounds—this time in his regular
pants, a blue woolen sweater that Esther had knitted for him, and
his topcoat—alone in the backseat.

It was a beautiful day for a baseball game—sunny, blue skies
occasionally broken by puffy clouds, a slight breeze and a tempera-
ture of 59 degrees, according to the radio weatherman that Jake listened to every morning on WHN before he set foot outside his door.
Not like the first two games at the Stadium. Then overcast skies,
light rain, and temperatures in the 40s cooled thoughts of any pro-
longed Indian summer while the Babe chilled any plans the Giants
had of surprising the Yankees in their home park.

He had read about it in the newspapers. Not just the *World*
which had its usual complete inning by inning coverage, but in the

Forward—page one stories highlighting the way Ruether and Hoyt toyed with the Giants' bats while Ruth and Gehrig led a home run barrage against "Ginsberg and Schwartz's team," sending them to two lopsided defeats. There was even a special editorial by Abe Cahan in Friday's paper—the day after Yom Kippur, the day after the second game when Hymie announced that he would not play because it was the holiest day in the Jewish year, the day that he and Morrie, who was not scheduled to pitch until Saturday, went to synagogue with Jake and stayed there from sunup to sundown—praising the faith of the newly discovered Jewish catcher who made his people proud by putting his religion before his profession.

"Tomorrow," Jake read aloud from the same column as the Packard bounced over the potholes on Eastern Parkway headed for upper Manhattan, "with Philly Schwartz behind the plate and Morrie Ginsberg on the mound, the Giants, with God's blessing, will triumph. It is as it should be. Jewish boys who know who they are, making their mark in America's National Game are living proof that the struggle to succeed in this country, while not without obstacles, is worth the fight!"

"What is happening to our socialist editor?" Max scowled. "Has he forgotten what it is like to work in a place like Mendelsohn's? Sounds like something you should read in the *American Hebrew* but not in the *Forvetz*."

"It's like that story about Benny Leonard," Jake responded. "He changes his name from Leiner so his parents won't find out he is a boxer. One night, long before he became champion, he comes home with a black eye. 'What happened?' his father asks. Benny, the story goes, can lie no more. He tells them he got it in a fight and then gives them a $20 bill—what he got for winning. His mother cries but the father, a tailor like us, picks up the money and tells Benny to keep on fighting. 'It's worth getting a black eye for $20,' he says, 'I am getting verschwartzt for less money each week.' What do you think Shlomo, have you heard that story before?"

"Everybody knows it Mr. Ginsberg. It's part of what makes Benny such a hero."

"And maybe Morrie, too," Max added, casting a glance at his own son's eyes fixed on the road in front of him, a son unwilling to be baited by his father's sarcasm even as he rehearsed in his mind what would happen on Thursday, assuming the Giants were still alive.

23

"NOW MEN, IT REMAINS to be seen what kind of stuff we are
made of. Forget about the first two games. We are in our home park,
the crowd is on our side today. Just play hard, bear down, and don't
let the big fellow hurt us," this last comment pointed by McGraw to
his Jewish battery, seated together at the end of the bench of Giants
huddled in front of him—a minyan of two in a minion of Gentiles,
all dressed in their home whites, each in their own way preparing
themselves inside for the battle ahead.

"All right, you heard the General, let's go get the fuckers,"
Hornsby piped in, up first, mouth already full of tobacco, juiced and
out the locker room door, his troops behind him, Morrie and Philly
bringing up the rear.

The long walk from the center-field clubhouse to the first-base
line where the Giants lined up for the playing of the National
Anthem did nothing to ease the tightness in Morrie's stomach.
Standing between Schwartz and Ott, he scanned the boxes directly

behind the Yankee dugout, half hoping that the object of his search would not be there. But there he was, his father, alongside Max and Shlomo in the first row, just where Shlomo had proudly insisted the seats would be, right in front, he noticed, of Davey Weiss and some well-dressed gentleman with whom he was deeply engaged in conversation.

Was that his father nudging Max and pointing to Morrie on the mound as he lined up next to his Giant teammates? What was with him anyway? Rosh Hashanah had been full of surprises, not the least of which was the way in which Jake had welcomed him home and said nothing about Doris. And he actually seemed excited about coming to the game today. "As if I need more pressure of being the stopper against the Unstoppables," Morrie wondered, "especially after the way they took apart Hubbell and Benton in the first two games."

The Babe also peered into the boxes behind the Yankees' dugout from his perch next to Miller Huggins right at home plate, but found only his friend and agent Christy Walsh, as it had been at the Stadium, alone with an empty seat next to him, next to Davey Weiss and Arnold Rothstein. His father hadn't shown up for the first two games, hadn't answered his wire (someone had signed for it at the tavern, he had checked on that), hadn't called, hadn't acknowledged sixty home runs, hadn't done anything any different than he had come to expect over the years since he left Baltimore on his own to make his way in the world. But something was different this time and Babe knew it.

[Alright, what did I know? What are your options here? Different wouldn't be me being pissed off about George Sr.'s absence, his failure to acknowledge me as a competent man, his inability to put his arm around me and tell me that he loves me. That was par for our course. Psychologically speaking, some might even say it's what made me who I was—larger than life, flamboyant, the biggest—you know, angrily striving to be the best in a futile attempt to gain his approval and at the same time to rub his face in my shit to let him know how angry I was at him for denying me what a son should expect from a father; sort of a modified Catholic version of "What Makes Sammy Run?" Or would different be blaming myself for his not showing up? What did I do wrong? When did I do it and did I do it over and over again? What did I do that would make my own father abandon any caring interest in his flesh and blood? Or did he, in his mind, abandon anything, or think that I did something wrong? Or does it matter, if that's what I understood to be the case? A conundrum of questions that build on each other but not, at least on the unconscious level, anything new to me. Or is it that. . . . No, wait a minute! You've got to be kidding. An epiphany for me! From what? One conversation with Davey Weiss?]

———

Babe wasn't surprised that the seat was empty. Nor was he angry. At that moment, he simply had no expectations nor any pain in their not being met. Whether or not George Sr. was there, he was still the Babe, the greatest baseball player in the history of the game and a decent guy to boot. "A prince of a fellow! Shit, a veritable Prince. . . .The Prince of Pennants? Pokes? The Prince of Power?" he mused, trying to find a ring to go with all his other handles, as he took in the scene, hat held over his heart, muttering the words of the Star Spangled Banner even as he eyed his Giant opponents engaged in similar song.

There was McGraw, as always in his white linen suit, too choked up with phlegm to manage a word; Hornsby, Terry and Jackson next to him, all looking stiff and tense, as they should be. And at the end of the line the two Jew boys, Taylor or whatever his new name was and the Ginsberg kid, who, he noticed, intently stared into the stands behind the Yankee dugout apparently in search of someone.

"Hope he has better luck than me," Babe thought, shouting encouragement to his teammates as the anthem ended and the crowd settled back into their seats, "Let's go boys, they're ripe for the taking and I'm ready to go."

Morrie wasn't but he had no choice. On the mound, he had thrown his last warm-up, received pats of encouragement from Jackson and Lindstrom—even Hornsby hustled in from second base to tell him to bear down—but now, looking into home plate, focused on the caged face and mitt of his favorite Jewish catcher as Earl Combs stepped into the box, it was time to face the music. What tune would be played remained the question.

"We'll make history today," Philly had told him before Mac-Cafferty, the home-plate umpire, broke up their conference on the mound.

"There never has been a Jewish pitcher and catcher in the same game before, World Series or not. No one expects much, not with the Yankees already up two games, and not from two Jews. So relax, follow my signs, and we'll bring home the bacon. Take them one at a time. Pitch Combs low and away, just follow my moving glove."

At least for the lead-off batter, the strategy worked. Batting from the right side, the lean six-footer watched Morrie's first pitch bounce in the dirt a good five feet from home plate before leaning into a fast ball that cut the corner above the knees. If the "Kentucky Colonel" had been a second more patient, the Yankees would have had an early lead—instead Combs lined out to Jackson at second base. Mark Koenig, the Yankees switch-hitting shortstop fared no better, bouncing out to Terry just inside the first-base line. Although Philly shouted encouragement as Gehrig stepped in, Morrie didn't know whether to be pleased or horrified. Always a slow starter, it was too early to know whether he had his stuff.

Gehrig provided a partial answer. The Columbia strong boy laced Morrie's first pitch off the right-field wall. It carried with such speed and force that Mel Ott, who had been playing regularly over the last two weeks of the season, covered the carom quickly and held the Yankee first baseman to a single, setting the table for the Sultan of Swat's first at bat and the stands abuzz with anticipation.

"Kayn aynhoreh!" Essie cried as Ruth strode to the plate, "Look at the size of him. Even from way up here, he looks very big."

Doris, wedged in between Essie and Esther in second-tier right-field grandstand seats halfway to the façade, nodded in agreement. She had been surprised when they called, didn't have the heart to tell them that Morrie had gotten her a seat in the lower boxes, and telephoned Philly right away who had managed to secure seats for them together, as it turned out not far away from where Esther had first watched her son play baseball. Then she knew nothing about

the game. Now, thanks to Abe Cahan, with her newfound knowledge, she could barely stand to look.

Shikey Friedman had no such problem. Twenty rows back behind home plate, flanked by Izzy Cohen, he had a good feeling about
the day and a fine view of Rothstein and Weiss. So far everything
had gone according to plan. Weiss had delivered the money—
$40,000 in denominations under $100 right on schedule. That gave
him a total of $50,000 to work with. Already he had laid down
$10,000 on the Yankees to win the Series and $15,000 for Ginsberg
and the Giants to win game three. The rest he held in reserve for
Thursday's big pay day, if it came. Somehow he knew it would. And
with only a few people involved, little chance of 1919 all over again.

Except for one thing. 1928 was 1919 all over again in one very
important way and Arnold Rothstein, comfortably seated next to
David Weiss, his topcoat off in the warming sun, neatly folded on
the empty seat between himself and Walsh, knew what it was. It was
him.

"What do you think, David, will Ruth touch one off and put the
Giants out of their misery early?"

"What would be best?"

"It doesn't matter. Everything is taken care of. We only have to
sit back and enjoy the day."

"You seem very calm about...."

"David, enough talk, especially here," whispered Rothstein. "I will
fill you in with all you need to know later, but rest assured that everything is well in hand."

That's exactly how the Babe felt as he strode to the plate.

"Well lookie who's here, Morrie. It's the keeed himself. Your Sultan of Swat, sometime saxophone player, the man you've only met at the Blossom Heath. Give him something he can hit. We wouldn't want to disappoint all these people who've come to see him, now would we," Philly cajoled, as Ruth entered the batter's box, took a couple of practice swings, and settled in, hands low on the handle, bat erect on his shoulder, cork-screwed power ready to unload on anything delivered.

Schwartz's chatter brought a smile to the Babe's face. "Anything will do, Zackala, as long as the kid keeps it in the park."

"Gevalt, the man speaks Yiddish. Who would have thought it," Philly responded, looking into the dugout at McGraw before flashing a sign to Morrie who waited nervously on the rubber.

McGraw's orders were crystal clear. "Walk the Babe, don't let the big fellow hurt us," and Morrie obliged, throwing four pitches well outside even as the fans, both Yankee and Giant rooters, voiced their disappointment about the denial of their pleasure in seeing the greatest hitter in baseball take his cuts.

"I'll catch you next time, Mr. Ginsberg," Babe called out to Morrie as he trotted down to first base, vacating the batter's box for Tony Lazzeri, who stepped in on the right side.

The book on Poosh 'Em Up was wide open—pitch the hard-nosed second sacker outside and you were in good shape but give him anything inside, over the plate or not, and you risked having your head taken off with line drives back through the middle that had become the trademark of every Italian's favorite ballplayer.

Although Philly remembered the lesson well, Morrie, bathed in sweat but relieved to have escaped Ruth, forgot to stay on the same page. The result was a screaming liner over the mound that drove in Gehrig and left men at the corners with Pat Collins due up.

"Time," Philly demanded, and hustled out to the mound while MacCafferty dusted off home plate.

"What's the matter Morrie? Calm down! Don't be so nervous. Just watch my signs and aim for my glove. We'll be out of here in a minute. Collins can't hit anything around the knees. Let's hog tie him and go to bat, Whaddya say?"

Morrie nodded, turned his back to home plate, stood off the rubber, Spalding in hand, eyes turned up towards the center-field clubhouse where Jewish fans and Giant teammates had carried him triumphantly only a few weeks earlier.

"What is Morrie doing?" Esther insisted, watching her son's every move. "Where in the *Forvetz*, Essie, does it say that standing and staring is something you should do? It looks like Morrie's praying."

"And from the stands and bleachers, the cry of Oy, Oy rose,
For up came Morrie Ginsberg, half a foot behind his nose."

No ancient chants, rather lines from the poem that so infuriated his father echoed in Morrie's ears, immediate reminder of a triumphant, communal moment that brought its own disappointment and rage.

"Play ball," MacCafferty demanded.

And Morrie did. His first pitch to the Yankee catcher sailed towards his head and drove him off the plate, into the ground. The next delivery, right on his catcher's target, changed up a few inches below Collins's knees. He tapped a feeble ground ball up the third base line that Freddie Lindstrom handled easily, his throw reaching Terry a good three steps before the Yankee batter made it to first base and only a few strides before Morrie crossed the first-base line and headed into the dugout to await his team's turn at bat.

Whether it was God's confirmation or Morrie's determination, the absence of a sinking curve ball from Urban Shocker's usual bag of tricks, or the swinging bats of desperate men buoyed by their hungry fans, the Giants quickly followed their pitcher's suit. Hornsby and Jackson punched singles over second base and Freddie Lindstrom walked, setting the table for Bill Terry.

"C'mon Billy, tie into one," McGraw urged from the dugout, barely heard at home plate over the hum of the crowd as the Giants' first baseman stepped into the box. Handcuffed the first two games by Yankee pitching, the lanky batter stood back in the box, content to wait until Shocker fell behind in the count and came in with the right pitch. It never happened. Terry walked on four straight pitches, Hornsby touched home plate, and the Giants tied the game. Three pitches later, while Wilcy Moore quickly began to throw in the Yankees' bullpen, Mel Ott cleared the bases with a shot into the left center-field stands that the Babe never had a chance on. By the time Morrie began his second inning warmups, the Giants had chased Moore as well and led 7–1.

"I know, I know, it's a piece of cake, a walk in the park, or as you would have it today, a pig in the poke, right?" Morrie asked Philly, who had joined him on the mound.

"I'm glad to see you're loosening up," Schwartz smiled. "Now just aim for their kishkas and my gloves and we're in like Flynn!"

"Enough already. Just get back there and give me something to throw at!"

Philly obliged and Morrie stayed on his game. Ruth touched him for a double his next time up but with the Yankees down 9–1 in the sixth, Huggins rested the Sultan and conceded game three. By then Jake and Davey Weiss were on a first name basis, Shlomo and Arnold Rothstein acknowledged each other, and Max and Christy Walsh began unauthorized negotiations for Morrie and Philly's vaudeville debut.

"Will we see you tomorrow, Jake?" Weiss asked, preparing to leave for the Blossom Heath as Ott strode to the plate to lead off the bottom of the seventh.

"If God and the Giants are willing, our next scheduled visit is to Yankee Stadium for the seventh game, right Shlomo?"

"That's right Mr. Ginsberg. To see Morrie pitch."

"Well, I hope we meet again. Either way, you and your boy are always welcome at my inn. Tell Morrie I said hello." And with that Davey waved good-bye to the others in the box, whispered something in Rothstein's ear that brought a smile to his face and made his way up the steps to the nearest portal.

By the time Philly grounded out to second to end the inning, Walsh and Rothstein were ready to leave. "Good to see you again Mr. Goldstein," Rothstein nodded to Shlomo, unaware that Fats had a real name until this afternoon but discreet enough not to embarrass him in front of his father or disclose the true nature of their business relationship.

"Yeah, it's been fun to meet all you folks," Walsh added. "Tell the boys to give me a call, Max. I mean business now. I'm sure we can work something out. At the least I know people who can book them at Grossinger's! Especially if they can sing 'My Yiddishe Momma.'"

"Not a problem Mr. Christy. I will talk to them."

"What's all this talk about show business?" Jake asked after Walsh and Rothstein had left the box. "It isn't enough that Morrie plays baseball to make a living?"

"It was just talk, Jake, just talk. A way to get through the afternoon sitting in the same seat with one of New York's finest criminals and one of Babe Ruth's best friends. Besides, maybe something good can come from it."

"This from my socialist father," Shlomo retorted in perfect mimicry of Max that caught his father by surprise and sent the three of them roaring with laughter, together, feet propped up on the front rail of the box, setting sun still warm on their faces, awash in the flush of expectant victory and a moment of familiarity less and less familiar between such fathers and sons.

"Tell us the joke so we can laugh too," Essie insisted, as she, Doris and Esther settled into the now vacant seats behind these menfolk that they had eyed since Davey Weiss first left.

"Essie, Esther . . . what are you doing here? How did you get tickets?" Jake exclaimed, taking the words out of Max's mouth as the two of them nearly fell out of their seats.

"What? Only a father should see his son play baseball? Doris asked Philly for some extra tickets and he obliged. So here we are."

"I'm glad that it was possible. Thank you Doris," Jake replied, squeezing Esther's hand. "Such a day, Mama, Such a day!"

And so it was. For Morrie, for McGraw, for Jake, for Esther, for Shikey—exciting and important as its own moment and possible prelude to a more momentous one, assuming the Giants could keep on winning. Which they did, for the most part.

Hubbell picked up where Morrie left off, shutting out the Yankees, only the third time all season they hadn't scored a run, while Hornsby and Ott provided a three-run cushion. Although the Giants dropped the fifth game at home when Benton fell apart in the sixth and the Babe and Gehrig launched back-to-back bleacher shots—Ruth's with two men on—Fitzsimmons surprised Murderer's Row in their own park with a three-hitter that deadlocked the series at three games each.

Through it all, Esther and Essie sat huddled around Esther's kitchen table, drinking tea, eating mandel bread, and keeping score by following the directions provided in the *Forward* with graph paper and pencil purchased at the corner candy store. Jake and Max joined them for the Sunday game but otherwise listened on the radio that Max brought from home, set up between their machines at full volume barely heard over the Singer hum and clatter, but permitted by Mendelsohn who feared that his two best workers would walk out if he did not allow them their American fascination.

Shikey Friedman had a better seat, be it in the Polo Grounds or at the Stadium, ever confident and richer as the games unfolded, anxious and ready for the seventh game. Shlomo, too, if not as certain about the outcome or his own feelings about it all. McGraw and Ginsberg, each from their own perch on the Giants' bench. . . .

———————

——

[O.K! We get the point. What is this—*West Side Story*? Anita, Tony, Sharks, Jets, Maria—each anticipating what the night will bring—soliloquies tied together by common purpose permitting feelings to be expressed while at the same time carrying the story forward. I think not! On the other hand, I've got to hand it to you. The seventh game cliché works. I had my doubts at first, but let's face it virtually every baseball novel is a cliché in one form or another. God knows how many of them end in seventh games or some similar do or die situation. It's an accepted convention. I buy that, even if it means there's less attention to the incredible series I am apparently having, based on the little bit you have mentioned.]

———————

———

. . . found their own visions to ponder. For the Giants' manager, a Series win would be the moment on which to retire. To Pennant Park. To the warm Februarys of Sarasota. Relief from the harsh New York winters that scourged his sinuses. Fishing, golf, afternoons at the track, just like the poster with his picture on it claimed. He and Mary already were building a new home down there—money advanced by the local banks on his reputation and his own substantial investment in the development of the place. One more win and he could cash it all in, in more ways than one.

For Morrie, beginnings were more in order—with his father, Doris, as a baseball player, with himself—visions all tied to the seventh game at the Stadium, the House that Ruth built, lived in, and dominated like no other ballplayer ever had in any other ballpark.

◇

24

MAX AND JAKE WAITED on Jake's front stoop for Shlomo to pick them up—on the steps where Morrie had honed his accuracy and power by bouncing spaldeens off its concrete cracks and risers, surfaces unknown to mothers and fathers too busy with other things to pay attention to the intricacies of stoop ball. But they did not wait alone.

Babies in strollers with their mothers; old, retired Jewish men, widowed and with wives; some children, especially boys too "sick" to go to school—all came out of their identical brownstone houses, down their identical seven stone-stepped stoops surrounded by the same brown patches of earth that held an occasional evergreen bush or flower bed, on a warmish October morning to wish Morrie well— or at least his father. It was their day as much as Morrie's. So Abe Cahan had said that very morning in a front page story about Morrie and Philly—a day of celebration and expectation, a day to be proud that you lived on Sackman Street.

Morrie felt it too. "New York, New York. Population 1,800,000. The most important of the five boroughs that make up the nation's largest city. The entertainment and financial capital of the United States, known for its fine restaurants, museums, theatres. Home of John McGraw's New York Giants, perennial National League contender, led by Morrie Ginsberg, a young, brilliant pitcher, formerly from Brooklyn, now taken by the bright lights of Broadway, the lovely, warm body of Doris Smith, the chance for fame and fortune unknown to any member of his family, on the steppingstone of a new life in the New World of New York, New York. Population 1,800,000. . . ." This, his own contribution to the imaginary almanac that ran through his head as he awoke in the hotel room that McGraw insisted upon for all his players once the Giants clinched the pennant.

Embarrassed and thrilled by his private composition, he checked the clock, rolled back on his side and closed his eyes, hopeful for a few more moments of sleep or perhaps another peek at the power of his imagination.

"Here, Jake, some herring sandwiches for you and Max. Enjoy them!" this from Mr. Gitletz who owned the appetizing store on Powell Street.

A store well named—saw-dusted floors, full pickle barrels, dill and vinegar odors mingling with the smells of fresh rye bread, lox, herring, chubs, and whitefish to create a scent indescribably, well indescribably appetizing—this, Jake thought, as he placed the sandwiches in the already overstuffed basket of food that Essie and

Esther and prepared for The Day at the Stadium—tomatoes, a salami, hard-boiled eggs, bread, ruggalech and sponge cake.

"I will feed this to Mr. Ruth," Jake had joked as Esther orchestrated and arranged the food, "if he eats even half, Morrie will have no trouble today."

"Very funny, Jake, very funny!" Essie had intruded before Esther had a chance to respond to her husband's humor. "Just eat for the four of us, as if we were there too. Maybe we'll hear you chewing on the radio."

"Enough Essie," Esther had interrupted. "Today we will sit home and listen on the radio. It will be alright. It's nobody's fault that there were no more tickets."

And now they all sat on the stoop, surrounded by their friends and neighbors, waiting.

———

Waiting for Shlomo. Only blocks away now, on Pitkin Avenue, eyes fixed on the road in front of him, even as his hands tensed tightly around the steering wheel, going over in his mind what would happen after he picked up his father and Jake and headed off for the Bronx, what he would do when he got onto Mosholu Parkway and turned down Bennett Street. That part was easy. Mumble something about a wrong turn. Pull over to ask directions from a man in front of a warehouse and wait for Izzy and the boys to take over. What would happen after, however, remained to be seen.

———

"Hey Morrie, here's a letter for you that just arrived."

"Come on, Charlie," Philly scowled at the Giants' clubhouse attendant. "Hold the fan mail until after the game. We've got other things to think about."

"Alright, but the dame who gave it to me made me promise to give it to Morrie before the game. Said it was urgent."

"Thanks Charlie. It must be some last words of pitching advice from Doris. Go ahead Philly, I'll be out in a minute. I've got to go to the bathroom again anyway."

The advice Morrie received halfway through his last nervous piss before facing Murderer's Row in the House that Ruth Built was about pitching. But it was not from Doris:

———

happy new year. we have kidnapped your father and his friend. if you doubt us, look in the box behind the yankee dugout where they were supposed to sit. they won't be there. if you want to see them alive again you be sure that the yankees win. hit the first batter with the first pitch in the bottom of the second to show you understand. don't tell anyone about this, not even your kike katcher. kapeesh? your father certainly hopes so.

———

Unsigned, undated, letters unevenly clipped from newspapers and magazines into a frightening collage froze Morrie in midstream.

"What's the matter Ginsberg, you look white as a ghost. Shake it out and get out there and loosen up before we start the game without you," this from McGraw, cigar in mouth, emerging from one of the bathroom stalls several feet removed from the urinal where Morrie stood.

"God, I hope Mary was wrong," he thought. "Remember the last time you bet on a Jew," she had told him at breakfast. "You came home from Belmont unhappy and $2,000 poorer. 'Mary,' you said, 'they can't ride either.' Thank God she doesn't know the half of it. There's a lot more of our future and our money riding on this kid's arm than the old girl could ever imagine."

Surprised and embarrassed, torn between the letter's insistence on silence and his own need to share the news and seek instruction, Morrie meekly smiled, put the letter in his back pocket, pushed his member back into his trousers and buttoned up, unfortunately releasing more than a few lingering drops of urine that he had bottled up and that now lazily trickled down his pants leg, just like, he remembered, when as a little boy, he would forget Jake's instructions to shake after peeing to make sure he got it all out.

"Looks like you should have taken my advice, boy," McGraw laughed, noticing the growing wet spot on Morrie's pants. "Believe me. I've seen worse and done worse before a big game. Just forget about it and relax out there. I know you can do it."

With that, McGraw patted his pitcher on the back and guided him out of the bathroom, through the clubhouse and down the corridor leading to the dugout and the sounds, smells, and sunshine of a brilliant October afternoon, all the time offering words of encouragement to a young man whose mind was filled with thoughts far removed from curve balls and change-ups and who hoped beyond hope that when he took the field he would see his father and Max seated comfortably down the third base line behind the Yankees' dugout.

———————

———

"Shlomo, are you sure you know where you are going? This doesn't look like it did last week!"

"I know Mr. Ginsberg, I got off at the wrong exit. Don't worry. We have plenty of time."

Max grunted in disgust. Ever since that night at the synagogue, all the mixed feelings that he had buried about his boy when he first ran off had come back in spades; every word or action observed just another piece of evidence to be weighed as he struggled to come to terms with his own feelings about little Shlomo and Fats Goldstein. To be lost in the Bronx on a dirty, deserted street full of rundown warehouses was not the best way for his son to impress him.

"Go ask that man over there," Max insisted and Shlomo obliged, drawing the Packard alongside a solitary figure dressed in work-clothes, standing beside an open warehouse door. But instead of stopping, much to the surprise of his two passengers, he turned the car into the building while the man on the street quickly closed the door behind them.

"Shlomo, what is happening . . . ?"

"Don't worry, Mr. Ginsberg, nothing is happening. Please, you and Mr. Goldstein just step out of the car."

"I should have known," Max responded, who recognized Shikey Friedman's voice even before he came over to the car to hold the door open for him. In the meantime, Shlomo, silent since he pulled the car into the warehouse, slipped out of his seat and took his place near Izzy Cohen and several other men assembled in the dim light of the building.

"Known what, Mr. Goldstein? That you have lost your son? That you were right not to welcome him back? That you did nothing to deserve his love or respect? That. . . ."

"Enough Shikey," Fats screamed, "Just get on with it. This is not about my father and me, remember?"

"What is this about," Jake insisted. "What do you want with us?"

"Actually, very little, Mr. Ginsberg. We will simply keep you here for a day or so and then let you go home. That's all. Of course you will tell nobody what happened, that is if you want to see your Morrie again."

"But why, what is the . . . ?"

"Security, Mr. Ginsberg," Shikey interrupted, "just security."

◇

25

MORRIE SCANNED THE boxes directly behind the Yankee dugout, just as he had when he first took the field for his warmups. Still no sign of his father, Max, or Shlomo, although he could see Davey Weiss, Arnold Rothstein, and Christy Walsh together again. Strange bedfellows for his father and Mr. Epstein, he had thought, when Max and Jake told them of their wonderful afternoon at the Polo Grounds and Mr. Walsh's plan for a grand tour of the Catskills.

"'Ginsberg and Schwartz,' that's the ticket my friend Christy told me," Max told Morrie that evening when Morrie had returned home to see his parents and enjoy the flush of victory, again surrounded by family and friends but more fully than he had been only a few weeks earlier when his Giant debut had brought him to his mother's arms and his own tears.

His father laughed when Max spoke, not derisively as he had at "Ginsberg at the Bat," but lovingly, as lovingly as the embrace he offered his son the baseball player when he came through the door. If only he could return the favor today.

———————

[How noble and sentimental! Should we be reading in waltz time? Shit, for a minute there I thought I would become Morrie's father, metaphorically speaking of course—the role model for his future, the next entry in his almanac—the light in his Jewish dark- ness—however you want to phrase his recognition that it's O.K. to live fully, to enjoy, have fun, loop de loop at Coney, take a spin in a shiny new Ford, get between the sheets with shiksas named Smith, and not feel guilty about any of it. Or maybe. . . . No! Don't tell me! You mean the kid is going to have it both ways?]

———————

Thoughts of Mount Moriah flooded Morrie's head as he stood among the Giants, lined up along the third-base line in their trav- elling greys, flanked down the first-base side by pin-striped Yankees. But was he Isaac or Abraham and what were the parallels? Was he father or son—loyal follower or sacrifical lamb? And after all, Isaac wasn't sacrificed, only bound up and scared beyond belief, but never actually given up to prove his father's faith. It was the act of offer- ing not the offering itself that mattered in the end. But it wasn't God who was asking him to risk his father's life, only some punk who was out to make a buck by threatening to kill his father unless he made sure the Yankees won.

Make sure the Yankees won? As if he had some power to deny or insure it! Even if he had seen his father sitting in the stands, would it make any difference in how he would pitch? After winning the third game, he had felt confident about himself. Who would expect the Giants to win three out of four games and get to a seventh game? But as it got closer, as McGraw urged them on, herded them in and told them to avoid distractions, his mood changed. The lack of distractions, whatever they might be, had only heightened Morrie's fears about stopping the Unstoppables.

"Whoever is blackmailing me didn't have to go to all this trouble," he thought. "I'll be lucky to get out of the first inning alive. But if I do, what do I do then? If I pitch too loosely too fast, I'll be out of the game before I can do anything to control it, even if I could."

At least for the moment, Morrie's preoccupation required no action. At his best or worst, depending upon how you figured it, he could have some effect on the Yankees' bats. But if the Giants got hot at the plate, it might be a whole new ball game.

Dutch Ruether made it clear in the first inning that as far as he was concerned, that was not going to happen.

"C'mon Dutch, make it quick so I can hit," the Babe encouraged him as they took the field together to the cheers of thousands circling them in the open-ended stadium bedecked with red, white, and blue draping.

"Your wish is my command, O Sultan," the lefthander replied, slapping Ruth on the behind as the Yankee hero trotted out to his place in right field. From the first pitch to Freddie Lindstrom, a fast ball high and inside that sent the Giant third-sacker to the ground, Dutch took command of the game. Three pitches later Lindstrom was out on strikes. Hornsby popped a routine fly to right on the first pitch and Terry grounded out to Gehrig at first.

"C'mon Ginsberg! Let's go get 'em," McGraw implored, as his boys took the field. "Just take your time, watch the signs and stay on top of the game!"

"Stay on top of the game? What the hell does that mean?" Morrie wondered as he made his way out to the mound. Which games and how connected, that was his dilemma. In the balance hung the fate of the Giants and his father's life.

"Play ball Ginsberg!" came the cry of Harry McKay, the veteran umpire behind home plate.

"Yeah, Ginnzala, ready or not here we come," shouted Ruether from the Yankee dugout.

Shikey Friedman, impeccably dressed in a brand new double-breasted blue serge suit, a step above his usual cut, in line with the killing he had made on Ginsberg's last outing, felt good as he took his seat. Even his view was a better one than at the Polo Grounds—in the boxes behind the Yankee dugout, ten rows back and to the left from where empty seats framed by Weiss, Rothstein, and Walsh marked Morrie's trial.

Nothing would be official until the bottom of the second but Shikey was confident. He understood where Morrie came from even if he had removed himself from the same place. Always Morrie was a "good" boy—the kind that aunts and uncles always pinched on the cheek and "qu'velled" over. Sure, when they were kids, he lived in Nanny Goat Park and played ball until all hours—games tied to seasons—baseball, punchball, and stickball in the spring and summer, football in the fall and basketball in the winter and spring. And he didn't always bring home all the money he earned delivering groceries. After all, spaldeens, egg creams and baseball cards with that thin slice of bubble gum were not free. And those Dux jackets that Shikey envied for a brief time before his interests moved away from the school yard to more lucrative, if illegal games, cost something too. But Morrie, he remembered, didn't play hookey, was a good enough student, went to the cheder three days a week after school, and except when his father didn't want him to play baseball for a living, seemed to listen and respect his parents. No way, if he was on his game, would he risk his father's life. And if the note shook him up and made him a little wild, so much the better.

Similar thoughts with less clear outcomes shuffled through Morrie's mind as he took his windup and released his first pitch towards the plate—a called inside fast ball that ended up sailing over Combs' head and beyond the reach of Philly's outstretched glove.

"Time!" Schwartz called as he took a new ball from McKay and strode purposefully towards the mound.

"Alright, Morrie, what the fuck was that! Just take it easy out here. Don't think too much. Trust in God and me and everything will be fine!"

"What, no pork or ham lines today? Not even a little Yiddish flavor thrown in for good measure? I'm not so sure such inspiration will bring my fast ball down." Not what Morrie really wanted or needed to say but the best he could muster, unable to tell his friend the dilemma he faced with every pitch.

And not what his friend expected to hear. "Christ, Morrie. Cut the shit and pitch to my target. That's all I am asking."

Morrie nodded and kept his eyes on his catcher as he walked back to home plate. Philly, the Wandering Jew who had just returned to the flock, lost lamb reborn by trusting his heart and reclaiming his faith—and a better ballplayer to boot since he "cocked" Hornsby in the clubhouse. "Abraham it is," Morrie decided, at least for now, unless or until the Giant bats made him rethink his position or until his father took his seat.

The Yankees' center-fielder was the first to find out. Morrie's second pitch caught the inside corner of the plate for a strike, a sweeping curve that broke in at the last second but long after Combs had given up on it. Two fast balls later and Mark Anthony Koenig was on his way to the plate.

As he had since he got hot in August, the young man from San Francisco whom Huggins had installed at shortstop despite a weak glove, carried a shiny black bat on his shoulder—a Louisville special soaked in cottonseed oil, nicknamed by its owner as Cleopatra, glistening in the sun and as powerful as any mast wielded by Moses against the Egyptians as far as the Yankee skipper was concerned. But no match, as it turned out for the Giants' Abraham.

Koenig fouled off Morrie's first offering, a lazy pop-up that drifted just out of Philly's reach and landed gently in the empty seat before a surprised David Weiss, hot dog in hand—bus man's holiday fare—who picked up the spinning ball and put it in his pocket for his first ever souvenir at a ballpark.

"The start of a lucky day?" Rothstein laughed.

"We can only hope, Arnold, we can only hope."

Morrie, who followed the flight of the ball and witnessed its descent, took notice of Weiss but imagined his father, cigar in mouth, hands aloft, caressing the ball into his own hands, content and connected to every pitch that he threw.

An image that did Koenig no good. His next swing managed

only a meager ground ball down the first base line that Bill Terry easily handled.

"Atta boy, Morrie," the Giants' first sacker called out, as he fired the ball around the horn.

Morrie nodded his thanks, caught the lob tossed by Stonewall Travis Jackson, the Giants' steady shortstop, and turned to face his namesake, the Sultan of Swat—the Fabulous Splinter, the Prince of Ash and the King of Crash, Everyman's Icon—Ruth himself.

The Babe strolled to the plate, nodded politely in the direction of the Giants' dugout, and tipped his cap to the fans in the front row boxes—his personal royal processional accompanied by a growing cresecendo of recognition from the thousands in the stadium who anticipated his every move—The Show within the show worth the price of admission itself.

He had been all business since he first arrived at the stadium. Not the typical one hour before batting practice when he could be assured of an audience of young boys eagerly awaiting their hero as much as their hero sought them. Game time was 3:00 P.M. but he had been at his locker a few minutes before noon. Long before most of his teammates filtered into the locker room, he dressed for battle, just as he had been first taught, by Brother Matthias at St. Mary's when the school one year found enough money to buy uniforms for their senior team.

"Now boys, I'll show you a trick. First you put on your shirt, then your sliding pants, and then your hose and socks. Then, like this, you take your pants, turn them inside out, place them in front of you, stick your dogs through the south end here and then roll them towards you, pant end and stocking together."

"Like my mother puts on her stockings," one young boy reminded the Brother, who, blushing at the thought, nodded in agreement.

"Then, when it feels right, take the other end of your knickers like this and pull them up."

That's what the Babe chose to remember as he prepared himself for battle. The moment, now, was at hand.

"Good afternoon, keed. We meet once again. Put the apple anywhere you want to. I'm feeling real good today."

Morrie grimaced in acknowledgment, stood off the rubber, fully sweated, arm loose, aware after only two batters that he was in his rhythm—whatever that was worth against the game's greatest batter. "Stick to your plan," he told himself, unleashing a fast ball that whizzed by Ruth into Philly's glove, a rocket strike that the Babe disdainfully let pass.

"That's my boy, Morrie, That's my boy. Lay another one in the same place for Mr. Ruth here," Philly shouted, returning the ball to his battery mate.

Following orders, just like McGraw and Schwartz told him, Morrie did, catching Ruth by surprise; fully expecting a change-up or a slow curve, Ruth swung late with such force that his legs seemed to curly-cue around each other as he lost balance and fell ungracefully in the dirt and chalk dust.

Now it was no great thing to strike out Ruth. Every year he led the Yankees in that category. Counting the first six games of the Series he was pushing 100. But it wasn't a smart thing to embarrass him in front of his fans, especially when the chips were down. Schwartz knew it and Morrie, who watched the Babe as he slowly came to his feet and carefully brushed the dirt off his trousers, was about to learn.

"Try me again, boy," Ruth calmly requested.

"What, are you crazy? Not on my watch," Philly nervously laughed, calling instead for a waste pitch, outside and low towards the right side of the plate, just to take the steam out of the air. The King of Crash would have none of it. Stepping across the plate, he brought the bat down in a swooping arc off his left shoulder and caught the ball flush on the letters, sending it in a high loop down the left-field line and into the stands before he had taken more than five steps out of the box. Without a word, he circled the bases for the sixty-third time that year, as always, home or away, to the shouting voices of standing throngs who came out to marvel. Crossing home plate, the Bambino stopped and once again tipped his cap to Morrie, who, at least for that brief moment, forgot about his own worries, both as pitcher and son, and marveled too.

Shikey Friedman relaxed. "Nicely done," he thought. "Sharp for the first two batters, embarrass Ruth, and then serve him up a home run that everyone would expect anyway. A one-run cushion and we're only in the first."

"Forget it Morrie. My fault. We should have tried him a third time," Philly suggested as he placed the new Spalding in his pitcher's mitt.

"Are you kidding? If we did, the ball would have cleared the upper deck."

"Now you're talking!" his catcher laughed. "A sense of humor amidst adversity, always, of course, with impeccable timing. That, a good fast ball, and a sinking curve will get us through this day. Let's see if it works on Gehrig."

The first pitch didn't but the second did. Columbia Lou let a high fast one go by for a ball then reached out and tapped a low curve down the third base line that Lindstrom fielded on the run, barely breaking stride as he threw over to Terry for the third out. Morrie crossed behind Lindy—everyone had been calling him that since Lindbergh made it safely to Paris—and headed for the dugout, a quick glance towards the stands confirming his worst fears. "One inning down and who knows how many more to go," he thought.

Tempted as he had first been to let Philly or McGraw in on his secret, his turn on the mound had changed his mind. At least while he was out there, pretty much in the groove, he had some control over the situation—matters of conscience and integrity aside—at least from moment to moment until the moment of truth arrived. But what if he spilled the beans and McGraw pulled him? Would his replacement necessarily fare any better than himself? And if he didn't, what would happen to his father? Better, at least for now, to say nothing and see what happened.

"THIS IS WORSE THAN sitting on those hard wooden seats outside," Esther insisted as she got up to get another glass of tea from the pot warming on the stove.

"You're so right," Essie agreed. "There you can see what happens. Radio is good for hearing the weather and listening to The Ipana Troubadours but not for watching baseball. Nu Doris, what do you think?"

"I'm not so sure," she laughed. "Here it's nice and warm. Besides, I don't think they sell mandel bread at Yankee Stadium! You know, maybe the two of you ought to open a bakery."

"With what? and here?" Essie laughed. "Here on Sackman Street everyone already makes their own."

"But there are other places in New York besides Sackman Street, Essie," Doris responded, surprised at her direct talk, as if she were speaking to an old friend—one whose invitation to listen to the seventh game she didn't hesitate to accept.

Esther listened to her best friend and her son's new friend, entertaining now for the second time in only two weeks her first Gentile, not counting the Fuller Brush Man, Mr. Peters, who came around once every couple of months with some free item—a soap dish, some shoelaces—in the hope that she would purchase something more expensive from his suitcase—a more personal, if less familiar door-to-door service than that provided by Old Man Kaplowitz, who, once a week, peddled his "High Cash Clothes," offering cash for old clothing and always a chance for neighborhood gossip, which now included Morrie and this Doris.

How serious was Morrie about this beautiful, if strange looking girl, sitting at her kitchen table? He had never had a girlfriend before, not even a Jewish one, not even what the young people called a date. Dates she never knew from, except the kind once she ate at someone's wedding so long ago that she couldn't even now remember when. Jake had been the only man she had ever known and luckily the match her father had arranged back in the old country turned out better than many others she knew. But this was America. Full of baseballs, automobiles, radios, and shiksas!

"What do you think, Esther? Maybe we should think about what Doris has to say."

"Ssh, the both of you!" Esther replied. "I think that Ott fellow is coming to bat."

"What a day, Arnold! I wonder where my new friends Jake and Max are. I have news for them."

"News, Christy? Don't tell me you were serious about taking on Schwartz and Ginsberg as clients?"

"It's Ginsberg and Schwartz," Walsh corrected, " or, if I have my way, Ginsberg and Schwartz, McGraw's Jewish Roses! Win or lose, they're a sure bet in the Catskills. Jenny Grossinger wants them for Thanksgiving. First year they are staying open on weekends and holidays past the summer."

Weiss laughed. "And what will these tried and true entertainers do?"

"The details have yet to be worked out, but I figure the usual banter, poetry, and jokes unless there is some untapped talent, musical or otherwise, that I don't know about. I was hoping that Jake or Max could fill me in before I approached the boys."

"I'm sure they'll be here eventually Christy. It's only the first inning. Maybe they took a late train," Rothstein offered, his eyes drawn back to the diamond as Mel Ott stepped to the plate.

"You mean you haven't spoken to Morrie or Philly yet?" Weiss asked.

"Details, Davey, mere details. In this business you have to strike while the iron is hot."

Which was something neither the Giants nor the Yankees were able to do. Not that Dutch or Morrie allowed anything to heat up. While Rothstein watched, Ott became Ruether's next strikeout victim, one of five Dutch managed as he set the Giants down in order over the next four innings. Morrie pretty much kept pace, not as overpowering but in control—catching the corners and finding Philly's spots with consistent accuracy. To play it safe, he popped Poosh 'Em Up Tony on the arm with a soft curve to begin the second inning, just as the note demanded. Only in the fourth, when Babe drew a lead-off walk and Lazzeri moved him over to third with a one-out single, did he falter. Bob Meusel's sacrifice fly to center-field made it 2–0, which is where the score stood as the Giants came to bat in the top of the fifth.

◇

27

"THIS IS GRAHAM McNamee for the National Broadcasting Company hoping you all out there are enjoying this seventh and deciding game of the World Series. It's been one whale of a ball game sports fans. 2–0 Yankees, top of the fifth, Stonewall Jackson's coming to the plate. Let's see if the visitors can get something going. You know what I mean. . . ."

"If that fucking asshole says that one more time I'm going to smash this radio into a million pieces, YOU KNOW WHAT I MEAN?"

"Take it easy, Izzy. There's no need to smash anything. Things are going O.K., aren't they?"

"O.K! Tell me! What do you mean O.K?" Max screamed at his son. "It is not O.K., what you are doing, not any of this!"

"Shut up, will you. Be quiet and nothing will happen!"

"Your boy's right, Goldstein," Cohen added, now suddenly calm, an eerie smile on his face as disturbing in its own way as the rageful, taut redness that filled it only seconds before. "Just sit still and keep your big mouth shut, just like Jake here."

Standing was not an option for his father or Jake, tied together, as they were, back to back, in two chairs, ropes around hands and feet, immobile, except for their voices, in the middle of an empty warehouse presided over by Shlomo, Izzy and three new boys hired by Shikey for added protection. Not that Jake had thought about it. Nor, as Izzy reminded Max, had he spoken many words since Shikey Friedman had left for the Stadium.

"Max," Jake finally whispered. "This is not the place. Let it be, please. We have been through worse. Screaming at Shlomo will get us nowhere."

"That's right, Jake," Izzy continued, before Max had a chance to protest. "Fats here has nothing to do with what happens to you. It's all up to your boy. The Yankees win and you're O.K., provided you keep your traps shut about today. On the other hand, if they lose, so do you."

"Enough, Izzy. Shikey said not to say anything about anything. The less they know the bet. . . ."

Before Shlomo could finish, Cohen reached up, grabbed him by the throat, and smashed his head hard against the warehouse wall.

"You fucking chicken shit! Don't you ever tell me what to do! You understand? You do it again and I'll break your fucking head off! Now just sit still and listen to the ball game like everyone else."

Cohen let go and Shlomo slumped to the floor, bruised but conscious, conscious too of his father's eyes on him, Max's speechless disgust riveting him in his place more forcefully than anything Izzy had dished out.

———————

——

And certainly more forcefully than anything Giant batters could manage against Ruether in the top half of the fifth. By the time Shlomo regained his feet, brushed himself off, and resumed his watch by the radio, McNamee had counted Harper out on strikes and put Schwartz to bed on a ground ball to Gehrig.

"That brings Ginsberg to the plate. Not a bad hitting pitcher, fans. Batting .243 since he joined the big club, with two home runs and six RBIs. Let's see what he can do against the Yankee southpaw, If you know what I mean?"

———————

——

[That McNamee! What a voice! Commanding, that's what it was! And the radio! Shit, without it, there never would have been me. In 1920, when I signed with the Yankees, there weren't more than a few hundred sets in the entire country. It was a brand new invention, like the Model T had been in 1900. By the time 20,000,000 heard McNamee's voice—actually a good many of them heard Major J. Andrew White's on CBS—everybody had one—over $800 million in sales alone in 1927! Icons of Abundance—Culture for a New Age— the Model T., the radio and Me! Sure I was a great player. But do you think that Colonel Ruppert would have paid $70,000 a year or that Christy could have gotten me $1,000 a week on the boards, if I wasn't a household word? Can you imagine what I would be making today when journeymen .230 hitters pull down a million a year. Shit! it's beyond my math, if you know what I mean?]

―――――――――――

――――

"Back again, Mr. G.!" Benny Bengough greeted Morrie as he stepped into the box. "I was thinking that Johnny would have pulled you for a pinch-hitter this time around. After all, you boys are running out of innings."

Morrie, too, had wondered about the same thing. He was pitching well and McGraw knew it. But the Yankees were up two and looked rock solid behind Ruether. And when he came off the mound at the end of four and McGraw made it a point to come down the bench to talk to him, he was sure his day was over and his father's life in other hands.

"Don't worry about the runs, boy," his manager offered. "We'll get them back. You're doing fine out there. Just keep your head up and stay focused. That's the key. Like I said."

McGraw's confidence helped Morrie brush off Bengough but it didn't make a difference against Ruether. Dutch wasted no time with his opposite number. Two inside fast balls over the plate put Morrie in a hole. The big lefthander wasted the next pitch, a change-up that fell low and off the table, but paralyzed Morrie on a called third-strike curve that broke inside over the letters.

Morrie froze just for a moment at the plate, in grudging admiration for the painless mastery in which he had just participated, watching the ball Benny had rolled back towards the mound as Dutch strided off towards the Yankee dugout. If things stayed as they were, no matter how he pitched, the Yankees would win and his father saved. Or so the note said. But there were still. . . .

"Let's go Morrie," Philly interrupted. "Here's your glove. Get out there and keep them quiet. This thing's not over yet."

Morrie took his mitt, tapped his forehead with his index finger several times, looked, as he had every inning, for his father, and headed out to take on the bottom part of the Yankees' order. Which, as it turned out, presented no major problems. Bengough grounded out, Jackson to Terry on the first pitch, and Ruether didn't take the bat off his shoulder as Morrie struck him out on four pitches. Earl Combs managed a single up the middle but Marc Anthony and Cleopatra failed to advance him, although the shortstop's long fly to right field had enough legs to send Ott back against the wall before he pulled it in for the third out.

"Alright gentlemen, this is the inning. Make him work Stonewall," McGraw's last words of wisdom as he headed out to his post in the third base coach's box.

"Captain John is right," Hornsby shouted loud enough for everyone in the dugout to hear him, including Morrie who stood at the end of the dugout putting on his jacket to keep his arm warm in the now coolness of the late October afternoon. "Ginsberg is keeping us in there. Let's give him something to work with, huh? And when we win, dinner is on me at the Blossom Heath. Everyone orders what they want! Davey Weiss tells me he's putting in a new menu in our honor. Shrimp and lobster for those who want it, stuffed derma and matzoh balls for those who don't!"

These last words Hornsby directed at Morrie, delivered in full Texas drawl with a smile and a shrug of the shoulders as the Giant captain made his way to the on-deck circle—words and movements that caught Morrie by surprise but that had their intended result.

Laughter, from Morrie, from Schwartz, from Ott and the rest, up and down the bench—the tension breaker Hornsby had intended.

On cue again, Hornsby, on one knee, turned back to the dugout and fired a coda. "How's my timing Philly? Not bad for a Methodist from Texas, right?"

"Not bad at all Rajah," Philly laughed. "Now, just put your bat where your mouth is and we'll be alright."

"My intentions, precisely. As soon as Travis here, gets on base."

Which he did. Stonewall, that is. On Ruether's first pitch. Despite McGraw's instructions, which Jackson had every intention of following, until the last second when it just seemed to stand still in the air—a hanging curve ball, lined into left field for a clean single.

Ruether's first pitch to Hornsby let him know that his concentration had returned—a high, inside fast ball just where Bengough had called for it, that drove the Giants' captain off the plate and to his knees. Hornsby smiled, tipped his cap to Ruether, and looked down to McGraw for the sign. Little Napoleon, arms clasped over his chest, remained adamant in his position—wait him out and make him work. Which Rogers did. For three pitches, working the count to 3–1 before he stepped out of the box one more time to see if Muggsy had changed his mind.

This was the kind of baseball McGraw loved. Long ball hitters like Ruth and Gehrig, even Hornsby, were fine for the game he had to admit. People obviously enjoyed the long ball as well as the stupendous swings and strikeouts that went along with the big boys who were always going for the fences. The more home runs, the bigger the scores, the bigger the crowds. No two ways about it. But the thrill of the game, for him, still was in the strategy, the careful pitching, the calculated gamble—stealing, hitting behind the runner, suicide squeezes—the inside game that he had perfected as a player in Baltimore and that he preached as a manager even as he made his own concessions to popular taste and the power of the Babe. This moment called for the master's touch.

McGraw picked up Hornsby's stare and stepped out of the coaching box to make sure that Lindstrom also had him in view. Then, without hesitating, he reached down to the grass, rubbed his hands together as he came erect, touched the brim of his fedora and clasped his arms in front of him—the same motions he had gone through on the preceding pitch except for the reach to his hat.

And as he had on the preceding pitch, Lindstrom took a short lead off of first as Hornsby stepped back in to face Ruether. Dutch's slow curve proved ideal to McGraw's strategy. Lindstrom took off for second as soon as the ball left the pitcher's hand. Hornsby squared just a bit and stepped into the ball before it broke, driving it through the hole between first and second—a well-executed run and hit that left the Giants with first and third, no men out, and Bill Terry due up.

"Here we go Morrie, Here we go. Come on Bill," Philly shouted—first to his battery mate then out to the plate where Memphis Bill, long overdue in the Series, prepared to take Ruether's measure. Morrie didn't know whether to cheer or cry. Only in his wildest American fantasies, in those games off the wall at P.S. 184 or on his stoop, by himself, did he ever imagine himself in such a spot—pitching for the Giants against the Yankees—Christy Mathewson against Wally Pipp—or at the plate with the bases loaded in the bottom of the ninth—just like in the Frank Merriwell, do or die, win one for the home-team tales that he bought for a dime at the local candy store and snuck into the house so his father wouldn't see them and ask him why he wasted his money on such stupid things, did such possibilities occur. Then, there were no tough choices to make. Morrie was always the hero and the Giants always won. Not so today. And for the moment, the outcome was not even in his hands.

McGraw clapped his hands together, then reached for his handkerchief in time to smother still another bolt of cough and phlegm. As always, he flashed Big Bill the green light. Not just because it was the right thing to do, although Dutch was too good a pitcher to start off behind another batter. No, ever since Terry came to the club in 1923, even though they didn't always see eye to eye about everything, McGraw tabbed him as his most trusted and knowledgeable player—not another Matty, no one could ever take his place—but a man who knew his baseball and who you could count on in the clutch.

The roar of the crowd let Morrie know that Memphis Bill had come through once again, a line drive over Koenig's head that drove in Lindstrom, sent Hornsby to third, and Miller Huggins to the mound. Shikey Friedman did not join in the noise. Early contentment had given way to growing uneasiness as the afternoon lengthened and Ruether and Ginsberg matched each other inning for inning. "The bastard's keeping it too close," he thought, as he watched Ruether leave the mound and Huggins give the ball to Waite Hoyt. "If we get out of this inning alive, Ginsberg gets one more chance. If he fucks it up, it's time to call Izzy!"

———————

———

"Tell me Christy," Davey Weiss inquired as Mel Ott stepped in to face the Flatbush Mortician. "What happens to Babe's value on the vaudeville circuit if the Giants should manage to pull this game out?"

"Are you kidding, Davey? The Babe's golden. Not that it mattered, but sixty home runs took care of that. I already have him signed up for fifteen weeks at $1,000 per. And if he wouldn't insist on playing that all-star circuit against those nigger-league boys, I could lock him in for another ten. On the other hand, if the Giants do win, why, my friends Ginsberg and Schwartz could do alright. Why we might even book them into the Blossom Heath, heh?"

"For their debut, I insist! What do you think Arnold?"

"I wouldn't miss it for the world, David, but first there is the little matter of winning this game."

Which was Ott's intention too, if his first swing was any indication—a left-handed powerhouse of a turn that sent Hoyt's first pitch deep down the right-field line, curving foul behind the pole by a mere ten feet and bringing the Stadium crowd to its feet and a lump into Morrie's throat, his stomach already churning as it had that night in the Blossom Heath when he had first confronted traif in all its forms. Three pitches later, Ott settled for lesser status, his sharp ground ball to Koenig's left side deep enough to bring Hornsby around with the tying run, even if the end result was a double play— Koenig to Lazzeri to Gehrig. Eddie Roush followed suit to the other side of the infield, a slow roller towards first that Gehrig fielded and flipped to Hoyt for the third out. 2–2, bottom of the sixth, and the Babe due up.

————————————

——

"Did you get that Esther? That's 6 to 4 to 3 and 3 to 1. That's what Cahan says."

"I got it Essie," Esther replied, looking up from the makeshift graph paper score sheet in front of her on the kitchen table. "According to my boxes, Babe Ruth is the next batter to see Morrie. Gevalt!"

"It could be worse, Mrs. Ginsberg," Doris laughed. "At least there won't be any men on base."

"Did you hear that Esther? She's beginning to talk like us. Have another piece of mandel bread, darling. It's obviously good for you."

"I think I will Essie. Who knows what might come from such delectable fare."

"Fare, shmare. Just enjoy. On you it looks good, right Esther?"

"Sha, Essie. It's time for Mr. Ruth and Morrie," Esther's mind too full of her son and his game to consider all the possibilities barely masked in such banter. There would be time later to think about such things.

◇

28

NOT FOR MORRIE. Nothing to think about now except what he had been trying to avoid since he received that note in the locker room. If only it had been from Doris—a good luck message from his Gentile love spurring him on to victory, to warm hugs from his father, loving kisses from his mother, and their gentle acceptance of their son the baseball player and his shiksa girl, maybe wife, with little blond-haired, brown eyed grandchildren—Morrie Ginsberg: Jewish Frank Merriwell, God's gift to America, Emma Lazarus's litmus test. Not quite The Icon of Abundance but important, still, in his own way.

No time for such fantasies, not when the business at hand was morality and mortality—his own and his father's respectively. No time for much of anything, not with the Babe approaching the batter's box, McGraw's high-pitched voice urging him from the dugout to "stay focused" and his teammates infield chatter—"c'mon baby," "atta boy Morrie," "no batter, no batter," reverberating in his ears.

Morrie peered in for the sign from Philly, but now memories, no a specific memory, flashed instantly before him. "Time," he demanded of McKay, stepping off the mound just as the Babe settled into his stance.

Time to remember in an instant a childhood minute. Just back from the candy store with a fine Bering Plaza for his father, seated next to him in the front parlor overlooking Sackman Street on the only piece of furniture in their apartment that held two people together, a faded red velvet love seat with claw and ball legs that his parents had bought for $10.00 from the refinishing store on Pitkin Avenue, saving their money for six months in order to make the purchase.

"Do you want the ring, Morrie?"

"Yes Poppa."

His father took his small hand in his own and carefully slipped the gold paper ring with its red-raised crown over his pinky, draping his arm around his son, contentedly smoking his cigar.

"Poppa, where do people go when they die?"

His father almost choked on his own smoke. "From where does such a question come? Is this what you are discussing in cheder?"

"No Poppa. From last week when Mr. Goldfarb died, after you and the other men on the block carried his coffin through the streets and said prayers in the shul for him. Where did he go?"

"Ah, Mr. Goldfarb. He was a good, honest man who was true to what he believed. His body is buried in a cemetery in Brooklyn, near Ocean Parkway on the way to Brighton Beach."

"Is that where you will go when you die?"

"Why do you ask such a question?"

"I don't know Poppa, I just wondered."

"It is where everybody goes who belongs to our shul."

"Me too?"

"No Morrie. You will live a long life and then, when you are older, you will make such decisions for yourself. It is part of being a man, making decisions about how to live and where to be buried."

"I don't know if I want to get older."

His father stopped puffing then, took his arm from off his shoulders and turned and faced his son. "Of course you want to. Why would you not?"

"I don't know."

"Look Morrie, you are too young to understand what I am going to tell you but listen carefully and remember. Even when you are alone and you have to decide for yourself what to do—what is right and what is not—just look at your pinky. The ring will always be there. Your Mama and me will always be there. This house, this couch, this street will always be a part of you. Just trust yourself and you will be fine."

———————

———

[What do we have here? A didactic Mel Brooks parody? And may the Schwartz be with you too! Where does Jake have it in him to pull this off? Was 737 Sackman Street such a palace of virtue and warmth that Morrie would want to remember "the house, the couch, the street," "the Mama," to say nothing of "the Poppa"? Is this some half-baked version of *Fiddler on the Roof* that all your work has come down to? And what does it mean to "just trust yourself and you will be fine?" How is this piece of advice going to help the kid in his moment of need? I sense another epiphany coming!]

———————

———

A moment long forgotten and rarely repeated, especially as he got older and the distance between himself and Jake increased, along with the conflict and turmoil that marked and colored all of their existence. A moment that marked the richness of the life that he was leaving behind but that he would never forget. And advice that quietly affirmed his original talmudic decision to pitch his best, to offer ultimate sacrifices as a measure of his faith and trust—to "stay focused"—propelled Morrie's first pitch to Ruth, a fast ball, low and away, just as Philly called for and released with all the power he could muster from a man determined to pitch as his father had once instructed him to live.

And the Babe crushed it. The Bambustin' Babe; the Manlin Mandarin, the Great Gate God, the High Priest of Swat, the King of Klout, the Battering Bambino, the King of Diamonds, the Caliph of Clout, the Potentate of the Pill, Big Boy Blooie, The Sultan of Swat, the Behemoth of Bust, the Mightiest of the Maulers reached out, fully extended and caught the ball flush on the Spalding, driving it on an ever-arching arc, over Travis Jackson, over Mel Ott, higher and higher climbing past the third deck and out of the Stadium, still not at its highest point as it climbed out of sight to Morrie, to Philly, to McKay, to the spectators who had even a glimpse of the ball, and of course to the Babe, who stood at home plate, and watched, like everyone else.

Morrie kicked the rubber in disgust and kept his eye on Ruth as he chicken-stepped around the bases, cap raised to the crowd, a smile on his face, loving every second of his triumphant circle.

Which just goes to show how much you can count on moral certitude when you come up against larger than life matters, of which the Babe was clearly one.

So Philly suggested to Morrie when he came out to comfort his pitcher and settle him down before he faced the rest of the Yankee order. "What can I say, bubela, the man is very, very special. Be happy that he came up with nobody on. One run does not a ball game make. Let's get the rest of these goniffs, Nu?"

"That's fine by me," Morrie replied. Not only with words but with action. Released by Ruth's Ruthian clout, Morrie dispatched the next three Yankees in short order. Fast ball after fast ball, ordered up by McGraw and passed on by Schwartz, each with more hop and speed than in the early innings, found Gehrig, Lazzeri, and Meusel wanting. Columbia Lou struck out on four pitches, Poosh 'Em Up Tony smacked a hard line drive that Hornsby snagged on the run between second and first, and Long Bob took a third strike, hardly expecting a third heater down the middle after swinging late on Morrie's first two pitches.

Shikey Friedman slapped his rolled-up program into his hand and headed up the aisle as the Giants ran off the field. Ruth's home run had his juices up, but damned if one run was enough of a cushion in a game like this. And not the way that Ginsberg threw the rest of the inning. He had underestimated the kid, never thinking that he'd play with his father's fate. "Well, fuck him and his father! And while I'm at it, I'll have Izzy finish off Fats and his old man like we talked about. That'll give him something to do that he'll really enjoy," Shikey thought, as he waited impatiently for a man, back to him, to exit the only phone booth under the stands near his section.

"Come on buster, hurry up will you!" Friedman bellowed, banging hard on the booth's glass door with fist.

"Now, Shikey, there is no need to be so impatient, is there? After all, it's too late to change your bets, isn't it?"

"Arnold, I'm sorry. I didn't know it was you in there. Shit, I hope I didn't disturb you," a startled Friedman stumbled as Rothstein opened the phone booth door and moved aside.

"It is not a problem, Shikey. Please. Be my guest," Arnold responded, gallantly waving his right arm in the direction of the booth for Friedman to enter.

Which was the last thing the aspiring hoodlum from Nanny Goat Park ever did. In the instance of Rothstein's grand gesture, Shikey, himself, with no option but to enter, sensed that possibility. Before he could pull the door closed behind him, while Arnold Rothstein walked towards the concession stand where he had promised to buy hot dogs for Christy Walsh and Davey Weiss, both surprised by the offer from this man who was used to having people wait on him, men accustomed to playing that role carried out his latest whim.

Five large men, dressed very much in Shikey's style, surrounded the phone booth, blocking it from public view. Monk Eastman, Arnold's mentor and trusted companion, as powerful a hitter in his own right as the Babe was on the diamond, entered behind Friedman, grabbed him by the throat, placed the barrel of a muzzled .38 revolver deep into his chest, and pulled the trigger three times, rocking the phone booth almost off its moorings before it settled down again, the weight of Friedman's slumped shape providing the necessary ballast to the bullets' force.

Twenty blocks away, on a deserted, dirty Bronx warehouse street, virtually at the same moment, Abe Attell, joined by ten of his best men, carried out the rest of Rothstein's plan.

"I understand Arnold. We will be there as soon as possible."

With those words, despite graying hair and wrinkled forehead still as lean and tough as when he swept the docks of San Francisco clean on his way to becoming world featherweight champion in 1900, Attell came out of the only phone booth on the block and gave the O.K. to his boys to begin their assault on the building where Jake and Max were held captive.

It was a good thing for them that Rothstein called when he did, for at that moment Izzy Cohen, always impatient and not much of a baseball fan, understood that the game on which so much rode was much closer than it was supposed to be.

"Shikey should have called by now. Something must have gone wrong."

"Take it easy, Izzy," Fats responded, jumping up from behind the desk where he had been seated since his earlier dispute with Cohen. "The Yankees are still ahead and there are only a few innings to go before. . . ."

"Shut the fuck up. I know what to do. I know what Shikey said. Untie their feet and put them up against the back wall. Hurry it up!"

"Now wait a minute, Izzy, Shikey didn't say anything about killing anybody. That wasn't part of the deal. No one is supposed to get hurt, remember?"

"Remember this you scared piece of shit!" And before Shlomo

had a chance to duck, Izzy plugged him with a .38 slug in the right shoulder that shattered his collar bone, missing his heart by a few inches.

"Shlomo!" Max screamed as he watched his boy spin around and crash into the wall behind him.

Before he could say any more, before Shlomo had a chance to answer, before even Izzy had time to choose whether to finish off one Epstein before killing the other, a truck normally used to deliver the illegal beer that made up part of Arnold Rothstein's enterprises, complete with portals cut into its sides that afforded opportunity and protection for the gunmen it carried, crashed through the wooden warehouse doors and stopped just a few feet short of where Max and Jake sat bound. Or to be precise, at that moment, toppled over, as both men, still bound together, fell to the ground as they struggled to get out of the way.

Cohen was not so lucky. Izzy did manage to get off one more shot before one of Attell's boys machine-gunned him down from the truck, his bullet-riddled body falling over the desk behind which Shlomo still lay. The rest of the boys that Buggsy had hired offered no resistance. Professionals in their own right, they knew the score, and of course the men who now held them at their mercy.

"Take them outside boys," Abe Attell ordered, stepping out of his red Studebaker sedan that he had pulled into the warehouse behind the truck once the shooting had stopped.

"Is about time Abe," Shlomo moaned, "I didn't think you were ever going to get here!"

"I came as soon as Arnold called."

"Shlomo, you are alive! My God, I thought you were dead."

"Don't worry Pop, I'll be O.K. I took it in the shoulder not in the chest. Are you and Mr. Ginsberg O.K.?"

"We are fine, Shlomo," Max answered, "just a little dirty that's all. And as soon as Mr. Abe Attell finishes untying us we will take you to the hospital and get you fixed."

"You recognize me?"

"Who can forget a face like yours? Today everybody raves about Benny Leonard but I remember you when you were The Little Hebrew. Remember, Jake, when we saw him fight in the Garden. It was during the summer—1913 or 1914. You were making a comeback...?

"You mean the fight against Willie Beecher when I punched out the referee...?

"Enough of this for now. Come, Jake, help me with Shlomo. Mr. Attell, will you take us to the nearest hospital, please?"

"No, Pop," Shlomo interrupted, leaning against his father, his left arm draped over his shoulders. "Abe has to take Mr. Ginsberg directly to Yankee Stadium, unless it's too late."

"Too late for what, Shlomo?"

"I'll explain in the car Mr. Ginsberg. Come on, we are only a few minutes away. We must hurry."

◇

29

IN THE TIME THAT IT took the two men to drive to the ball park, Davey Weiss and Christy Walsh managed to finish the hot dogs that Arnold Rothstein brought them—Sabrett's specials with mustard and sauerkraut catered as always as at every New York ball park and emporium by New York's concessions king, Harry M. Stevens, whose name appeared on every napkin and cup in which he dispensed his food and drink. While they ate, Waite Hoyt mastered the bottom third of the Giants' order, barely giving McGraw pause about any decision to pull Morrie for a pinch hitter. And Abe Attell told Jake as much as he knew about why he had suddenly appeared at the warehouse, which was not much—only that Arnold Rothstein had told him to go there, that Fats Goldstein would need his help in rescuing his father and one Jake Ginsberg; which is, he explained, how Arnold always worked—that is never revealing his whole hand unless, of course, it was necessary—a way of doing business that, he admitted, he had picked up himself and used quite handily on several occasions.

"Enjoy what's left of the game. I hope your boy wins. I got a wad down on him," this in farewell as Attell dropped Jake off on the corner of Jerome Avenue and 161st. Street, under the shadow of the elevated—pennant-selling hawkers the only people on a deserted street awaiting the throngs whose cheers and murmurs Jake could hear as he entered the stadium.

On his way to the mound, as he had every inning since the game began, Morrie glanced over his shoulder towards the box where his father, Max, and Shlomo should have been sitting. Empty seats still. Earlier in the day they filled him with anxiety. Now they only steeled his determination and tested his faith, which, if Joe Dugan had known, might not have made him feel so embarrassed, striking out as he did on three fast balls at such a crucial point in the game.

"That's my boy," Philly yelled as he tossed the called third strike back to Morrie.

Benny Bengough shouldn't have bothered either. The Yankee catcher flailed at Morrie's first two offerings—smoke again, and then a swing way out in front of McGraw's called change-up.

"Come on Ginnzie," Hornsby shouted in from his position between second and first, "let them hit something, it's getting kind of boring out here."

Morrie paid no attention as he turned back to the business at hand, unaware that he had struck out four of the last five Yankees he had faced since the Babe had unloaded his prodigious blast. Despite his captain's request, Waite Hoyt became the fifth.

The Little Hebrew knew the ins and outs of Madison Square Garden and Sunnyside Arena but baseball and ballparks left him cold. Jake entered the Stadium behind the center-field bleachers, far from his appointed seat, and it took him all of the top of the seventh to find his way around to where he belonged, his passage further slowed by a police barricade hastily set up under the stands near a phone booth while several of New York's finest carefully removed Shikey Friedman from his last phone call. By the time he got there, Morrie had left the mound, disappointed again not to find his father in the stands.

Arnold Rothstein, sitting on the aisle, one eye on the field and one eye on the tunnel out of which Jake appeared, saw him first. The Big Bankroll said not a word, simply smiled, bowed ever so slightly, and graciously extended his right arm, escorting him to his seat.

"Mr. Ginsberg, it's good to see you. We gave up on you a long time ago. Where have you been? You've missed a very good game. Your son is doing very well . . . except for the Babe."

"I know, Mr. Weiss, I listened to part of it on the radio."

"Where is Max?" Christy Walsh asked. "The way things are going I'm ready to sign up your boy and Schwartz."

"It is a long story, but he had to take his son to the hospital."

"Is Fats, I mean Shlomo, alright?"

"Yes, Mr. Rothstein, he will be fine, as we will be, thanks to your help. And now let me ask you for one more favor. Is there a way that we can let Morrie know that I am here?"

"Arnold, what do you know that I don't know?" Davey Weiss joked.

Rothstein just smiled at Davey, a smile that reassured his old friend that everything was in good hands while Christy Walsh knew well enough not to pry any further.

"Don't worry Mr. Ginsberg, Morrie looks this way every inning when he goes out to pitch. But I will try to get a message to him. You just sit here and try to enjoy the rest of the game." With that, Rothstein left his seat, patted Jake on the back, and headed up the aisle in search of an usher.

By the time he found one, wrote a quick note, and slipped Morrie's messenger a five spot, Freddie Lindstrom had waited out Waite Hoyt, drawing a lead-off walk after fouling off four balls with the count 3 and 2. True to McGraw's call, Hornsby hit behind the Giants' runner, sacrificing himself while Lindstrom slid safely into second.

"What's the matter, Waitey? This ain't no morgue here. Heavy lumber's coming to get you," shouted out Hornsby as he trotted back to the dugout.

Not the most original taunt, Morrie thought, but on the mark. One on, one out, Bill Terry at the plate, Ott on deck. . . .

"Morrie, another message!" Charlie's words accompanying a ragged edged brown remnant of paper, the side of a discarded peanut bag hawked at five cents a piece, that he thrust into his hands as he sat at the end of the bench, Philly beside him.

"Not another note from Doris? Jesus, Morrie, she should know better."

Morrie ignored his friend and carefully unfolded the paper in his lap, frightened and hopeful of what he might find there. Hand-written words—"Your father is watching you"—brought him to his feet with such speed that he smacked his head against the dugout ceiling, almost at the same time that Bill Terry caught hold of a Hoyt fast ball and drove it deep to right field, over the Babe's outstretched glove and into the lower deck for a two-run homer.

At once everyone in the stadium was on their feet, a commotion of cheering, yelling, and carrying on that brought the Giants out of the dugout to greet Terry as he rounded third base, a pounding on the back, cavorting escort to home plate. All, that is, but Morrie, who stood on the dugout steps, peered back into the stands, and found his father looking right back at him with a smile on his face.

———————

——

[I don't believe this! What chutzpah! Or is it just your propensity for sophomoric, sappy pap? I mean it's one thing for you to have Morrie come to terms with his father and pitch his heart out as testimony to his love. It took me a few pages to grapple with that idea and I finally decided that while it's not my cup of tea, at least it is consistent with your obvious desire to present the array of choices about fathers and sons which this novel is about. But this last scene is a bit much. Even Steven Spielberg would have trouble with this "E.T." crap! Give me John Sayles, please!

On a more serious note, there's also the small matter of Terry's home run! Are you really going to pull out all the stops and let the Giants win? O.K., O.K., I'll have to admit it. In 1921 and 1922 McGraw's boys did take us in the Series. But we beat them in 1923 and with this team we were almost invincible. Shit, after the Giants lost to Washington in 1924 they didn't even make it back to the Series until 1933. We barely lost it in 1926 and then took it all in 1927 and again in 1928. As I've already told you, it's one thing to take some liberties with baseball history when you're writing fiction but, really there has to be. . . .]

Morrie waved his arm slightly and smiled back—the smile of the little boy he once was and that he could now be again—even as other matters demanded his attention as a man. One of which was most immediate—putting the Yankees to bed.

"It's all yours, Morrie! Wrap them up and take us home," Terry shouted, leaping into the dugout as Morrie turned around to the tumult of his teammates' arrival.

"I'll do my best, Bill, I promise I will. For the team's sake!"

"Sure, Morrie, whatever you say, just show them your best stuff," this, Memphis Bill's puzzled reply, as he walked to the end of the dugout and settled back to watch Urban Shocker take his warm-up tosses—the Yankees' new pitcher, installed by Miller Huggins even with only a day's rest but with the game and the Series hanging in the balance.

Shocker did his best to give him the opportunity. The big right hander took care of Ott and Roush in short order—successive ground balls gobbled up by Koenig and tossed to Gehrig that ended the Giants' comeback and turned things back to the top of the Yankee order in the bottom of the eighth.

30

"BUBKA?"

"No, dearie, it's 'bobka.' You like it, nu?"

"Essie, it's even better than the mandel bread. How do you get the hard chocolate drips to stay on the cake like that," Doris asked, pointing to the half-eaten wedge on her plate, its surface coated with the crumbs of her earlier forays into the now empty plate of mandel bread that had gotten her through the top of the eighth.

"Esther. Did you ever see such a thin thing eat so much cake?"

"I'm sorry, Mrs. Ginsberg. I didn't mean to. . . ."

But Esther only waved off her friend's remark, stopping Doris as she spoke. "Please, I'm glad you like it. Besides it's good to eat when you are nervous. And right now, I am plenty nervous too. According to my graph paper, in six more outs Morrie is the winner." Reaching for her own piece of bobka, she added, "Ach, it is easier to watch this if you are at the ballpark than to listen to it on the radio, do you know what I mean?"

"Yes, Mrs. Ginsberg. I know what you mean."

"You know what I mean, Morrie. It's like I used to tell Matty. One run is as good as ten as long as you stay focused. Stay with your fast ball unless I tell you otherwise. Alright, go get these son of a bitches!" These last words of advice McGraw made a point to deliver on the steps of the dugout before Morrie headed out to the mound.

He had a good feeling about this kid, this Jew who would be the exception to the rule. Six more outs and he could go out in a blaze of glory, and cash. Retire to Pennant Park. No more travelling, no more overnights on Pullman berths too cramped even for his stubby body, no more sweaty clubhouses with no air that drove his sinuses crazy. Sure, he would miss the game itself. But his memories would give him enough of that. Especially this one, if Ginsberg could pull it off.

Right off the bat, Earl Combs let Morrie know that it would be no walk in the park. True to his word, Little Napoleon flashed the fast ball sign to Schwartz who relayed it to Morrie. And he delivered it, hard and true, but just a hair off Philly's target on the inside corner—just enough for the Yankees' center-fielder to send a line drive over Jackson's head for a base hit.

Determined to follow suit, Mark Anthony dug his feet into the batter's box, wiped the barrel of "Cleopatra" clean, and stood ready to face Morrie while the Babe moved into the on-deck circle. Again,

McGraw stayed with the fast ball, again Schwartz gave Morrie the sign, and again Ginsberg delivered.

"Strike!" Harry McKay bellowed, as the ball crashed into Philly's glove, almost knocking the catcher off his feet.

"Atta boy, smoke him out Morrie. The Emperor has no clothes!"

The Yankee shortstop set himself again but the result was no better—another fast ball, same location, same speed—strike two.

"Time!" McKay called as Koenig stepped out of the box to compose himself.

"Hey kid, come here for a second will you," Ruth called out to his shortstop, meeting him halfway between the on deck circle and home plate.

"Listen Mark. I've been watching this kid for the last few innings. He's throwing nothing but heat and he's not wasting any pitches. Start your bat early. Make contact. You can do it!"

Which he did, barely—so far out in front of Morrie's next speed ball that it scarcely found the tip of his bat—the result, a spinning roller towards the Giants' captain—a tailor-made double play ball right at the Jolly Rajah that he eagerly scooped up and tossed to a waiting Travis Jackson at second base.

Who dropped the ball. Plain dropped it. Even before Earl Combs slid hard into the bag. Precisely as Doris reached for her second chunk of bobka. Right at the moment that Arnold Rothstein reached over and uncharacteristically hugged Jake Ginsberg around the shoulders. He dropped the ball.

"Son of a bitch," McGraw muttered as he made his way out to the mound, his mind already churning through the unenviable choices he faced, Schwartz on his tail, the Babe on his way to the plate. He could put Ruth on and not let him take matters in his own hands. Except that loading the bases with no out in the bottom of the eighth and Gehrig due up was hardly a good place to put his pitcher. Which brought up whether to stay with the rookie or bring in Fitzsimmons, who had been warming up in the bull pen since the top of the seventh.

"How's your arm, boy? Don't give me any bunk now, there's too much on the line here," McGraw asked, as he joined Morrie on the mound.

"It's fine. Really!"

"He's O.K., Mac," Philly spoke up. "I've never caught anyone who threw harder than Morrie is right now He's knocking the kishkas out of me!"

"We're talking about the heart of their order here, dammit—Ruth, Gehrig, and that wop Lazzeri—and it's still Mr. McGraw to you."

"Let me have a go at them, sir. We'll win the day," Morrie's Merriwellian counterpoint to McGraw's Irish slur and Philly's Yiddish qu'vell.

"Save the crap and go after Ruth. He'll be looking for the fast ball. O.K., give it to him but not where he wants it. And not every pitch. Change him up. Curve him. Work the bastard."

With these parting words, McGraw patted Morrie on the back and headed towards the dugout, leaving his Jewish pitcher and catcher to deal with destiny in the form of the Babe.

The Babe, still-life at home plate, eyes fixed on McGraw, Ginsberg, and Schwartz, prepared in his own way for the duel about to take place.

[You have McGraw right about one thing. The key to baseball is focus. Sure, I fooled around a lot at the plate—scanned the crowd, waved to the kids, joked with the umps. But when I turned to face the pitcher—when I was on my game, which was most of the time— I made it my business to forget about everything else except the ball and my bat. Reggie Jackson got it right a few years ago when they put him in the Hall of Fame, the other house that I built, so to speak. Anyway, here's what he said. I cut it out of the *New York Times*. "You gotta get everything out of your mind except that ball the pitcher's got in his hand and you're thinking of getting the barrel of the bat in the pay zone—on time! Get yourself together, you tell yourself. You got the pine tar on your hands. You mash down your helmet. You fix your glasses. You shift your body so your shirt's fitting right, not hugging you. You plant your feet in the dirt and make sure there's no stones. And now he's gotta throw. Now I'm in charge. He gotta be out there with it. He's right there! He's right there! Pow!" Aside from the facts that I never used anything on my bat handle but dirt, helmets didn't exist, and I had 20-20 eyes, the man's on target. Which is how I always tried to be when I went up to bat. Just thought I'd fill in your details, in case you had other ideas in mind.]

Carefully he set himself in the box, pulled at his shirt until it fit just right, adjusted his feet, placed the bat on his left shoulder and fixed his eyes on Morrie's hands, intent on following the ball in its every move from mound to plate.

———

Merriwell peered in to get the sign from Smith. Lodge, Harvard's menacing right-fielder and the league's leading hitter, steadied himself for the pitch. Bottom of the ninth, bases loaded, two outs, the count three and two to Harvard's best batter, and the Crimson down by a run. Twice Frank shook off his catcher. No fast ball or change-up here. No, only one pitch would do, Frank thought, as he waited for Smith to flash him the sign for the curve. When it came, he delivered. The ball spun out of his hand. In slow motion, Frank watched its arc as it twisted towards home plate, floating almost aimlessly in the air, dipping first to the left, and then, as Lodge readied to strike it, back to the right, past his outstretched, futile bat, and into Smith's glove for the third strike. Yale players and fans mobbed their hero, hoisted him on their shoulders, and paraded Frank around the basepaths. "Three cheers for Merriwell! You were wonderful Frank. You saved the day for Yale. Without you Harvard would have won the game," shouted his teammates.

"No, we all did it together," Frank modestly responded. "Oh, what a glorious day for Elis everywhere!"

———

But not on my first pitch, Morrie thought, nodding his head to acknowledge Philly's called fast ball, high and inside. Which is where he delivered it. No surprise to the Babe who merely leaned back and tilted his head out of the way as the ball landed hard into Schwartz's glove. Nor on the second, another heater that dipped past Ruth around the knees, squaring the count.

Combs and Koenig moved off the bags as Morrie set himself for the next pitch, a change-up that Ruth barely missed. Even so, his own momentum carried the ball deep down the right-field line, foul by a good twenty feet but enough to bring the crowd to its feet and send a chill down Jake's spine, and that of every other Giant fan, Jewish or otherwise, in the ballpark.

Morrie caught the new ball from McKay, put his glove under his armpit, and stood on the mound, rubbing up the Spalding as his eyes roved the stands between first and third. There was his father in his proper place in the stands. There was his friend and Jewish catcher behind the plate. There was the Babe, setting himself for the next delivery. "Oh what a glorious moment," he thought. "It's time, Mr. McGraw, it's time!"

Sure enough, when Morrie looked in for the sign, Philly flashed him two fingers for the hook, on orders, as always from McGraw, who knew that no Yankee had seen a curve from Morrie in the last two innings. Morrie towed the rubber, went into a full wind-up, wrapped his fingers around the ball, snapped his wrist and released the sphere towards the Babe. The ball spun out of his hand. In slow motion, he watched its arc as it twisted towards home plate, floating almost aimlessly in the air, dipping first to the left, and then, as Ruth readied to strike it, back to the right, past his outstretched, futile bat, and into Schwartz's glove for the third strike.

Except that it never curved twice. If truth be told, not even once. It just hung there, for eternity, while the Babe brought the full force of Black Betsy into it, driving the ball over Mel Ott's head, deep into the right-field stands, for his third home run of the game and a two run Yankee lead.

The rest, as they say, is history. You could look it up. By the time McGraw decided to bring Fitzsimmons in, the Yankees had picked up two more runs off of Morrie. Hoyt set down the Giants in order in the top of the ninth and the Yankees won the seventh game and the Series.

By the time Jake and Morrie got home to Sackman Street, there was not a piece of cake left in the house.

31

NOV. 5—ARNOLD ROTHSTEIN, who declared not long ago that he had given up gambling in favor of the real estate business, was shot, perhaps fatally, at 11 o'clock last night. The police do not know where the shooting took place. It might have been in a west side apartment in the Fifties, in a hotel room in that neighborhood, or on Seventh Avenue. Rothstein, though conscious, would not tell them. News of Rothstein's shooting spread quickly along Broadway. The man who was accused of "fixing" the famous "Black Sox" World Series in 1919 prided himself on his host of friends. Scores of them were in the corridors of the hospital within an hour. One of the first of Rothstein's friends to appear was David Weiss of the Bronx, the manager of the Blossom Heath Inn which Rothstein often frequented. . . .

Nov. 6—Arnold Rothstein, who is near death at Polyclinic Hospital from a bullet wound in the abdomen received late Sunday was shot because he refused to pay $303,000 lost two weeks ago in a record-making game of "high spade," the police said yesterday, adding that he had "welched" because he thought he had been cheated. Involved in the game, along with Rothstein, were Jimmy Meehan, Myer and Samuel Boston, Joe Bernstein, Martin Bowe, Tommy Titanic Thompson, George McManus, and Nigger Nate Raymond. Barely alive despite two blood transfusions, Broadway's greatest chance-taker was taking yet another chance. Confident that he would pull through and in his own way deal with his assailant, he refused to aid the detectives investigating the shooting. Cautioned that his condition was desperate, he faintly shook his head.

Nov. 7—Brief orthodox Jewish funeral services were held for Arnold Rothstein this morning at 10 o'clock at the Riverside Memorial Chapel, Amsterdam Avenue and W. 76th Street. The bronze coffin was wheeled into the chapel shortly before 9 o'clock. More than 200 friends and relatives attended the services and viewed the body. Among the first to arrive were the immediate members of the family. They included parents Abraham and Essie Rothstein, his brothers, John and Edgar, his sister Edith, and his widow Mrs. Caroline Rothstein. Mr. Rothstein's body was interred at Union Field cemetery in Brooklyn. Before he died, Mr. Rothstein dictated his will to his attorney, Maurice Cantor. He is reported to have provided liberally for his wife, family, and for his many friends. Keen speculation existed on Broadway on the amount of fortune left by the slain man.

Estimates ranged all the way from $1,000,000 to $10,000,000. The favored guess was $5,000,000, which took notice of the fact that Mr. Rothstein owned several apartment houses, owned ground on which others were built and owned and operated the Fairfield Hotel on W. 72nd Street, where he made his home.

———————

———

David Weiss took another sip of coffee and turned the page of his scrapbook containing the newspaper columns that told of his friend's death. Six years ago, and yet it seemed like it was yesterday. He could still see Abraham Rothstein, his impassive body seated in the first row next to his wife and children, not a tear shed or a shred of emotion shown throughout the service or at the gravesite through the mist and cold of a damp November rain. How surprised Arnold would have been, he remembered thinking, to find his father at his funeral—the man who had sat shiva for him thirty years before and whom he hadn't spoken to since. And how surprised Mr. Rothstein was when Murray Cantor, ten days later in the lawyer's Manhattan office, announced that Arnold had left his father $500,000.

Yes, the *World* was right about one thing, Weiss smiled, Arnold surely had been generous with his bequests. John McGraw never would have found peace in Sarasota if it hadn't been for Arnold. And I wouldn't be sitting here in this office—the full and outright owner of the Blossom Heath—if. . . .

"Mr. Weiss, it's time that we left. The traffic will be very heavy today."

"Yes, Harvey, I'm coming. We don't want to be late for this one, that's for sure!"

"Come on Esther, Shlomo is waking up the whole neighborhood with that horn!"

"Alright Jake. How do you like me?"

Jake laughed as he watched his wife primp before the parlor mirror, pulling up the collar of her new black Persian coat that Morrie and Doris had bought for her birthday.

"Esther, I have always liked you. If you mean the coat, it looks good on you. Now let's go before we miss the boat!"

And a boat it was—Shlomo's new four-door black, shiny, Coupe de Ville, double-parked in front of 737 Sackman Street, his father already ensconced as shotgun and Essie comfortably seated in the Cadillac's spacious leather back seat.

"It's about time already," Max growled, as Jake and Esther joined Essie, "we will be late for the game."

"Don't worry Pop, we have plenty of time."

"Shlomo, this is a beautiful car. Business must be good?"

"I can't complain, Max," the younger Goldstein responded, as he gently guided his new car in the direction of Pitkin Avenue. "The new show that Christy and I are backing opens next week. It's going to be a smash."

"Some country, huh Jake?" Max offered. "We can't find work and people are going hungry but still the show goes on!"

"It takes their minds off their troubles, Max, just like going to the baseball game does," Jake responded.

"What's it called again?" Essie interrupted.

"I told you Ma, it's Cole Porter's *Anything Goes.*"

"Is that the Jewish boy who makes all those songs?"

"No, Mrs. Ginsberg, you are thinking of Irving Berlin."

"Whatever. Give me Boris Tomashevsky any day."

"Whatever you say," Shlomo laughed, "but I'll send you two tickets anyway so you can see for yourself."

"What about Morrie and Philly? Any plans to take them around the Catskills again?"

"Morrie didn't tell you?"

"Tell us what, Shlomo?" Esther asked.

"It's not definite yet, but it looks like we've lined up Paul Gallico to write about their experiences in baseball and how to play the game."

"Not Abe Cahan?"

"No, Pop, he wouldn't sell outside of Brownsville."

"You mean a book that somebody would buy?"

"That's the idea Ma. What a country huh?"

"Drive, Shlomo, just drive. Or we will miss the first pitch!"

"Whatever you say, Pop!"

———————

———

"Mama, will we be able to see Poppa from our seats?"

"Don't worry shmugins, they will be fine seats. Right next to Bubbe and Zaide."

"Will Aunt Essie and Uncle Max be there too?"

"Yes, sweetie."

A concerned look came over the little boy's face. "Did you bring enough cake for everyone?"

Doris tapped the large mint-green, brown-lined, white string-tied Ebinger's box sitting between them on the front seat as she headed across the Willis Avenue bridge towards upper Manhattan. "Are you kidding, there's bobka, ruggelech, linzer tortes and jelly donuts galore in here."

"Did you make them yourself, Mama?"

"Not this time, dear," Doris laughed. "I picked them up at the store last night." But not an unreasonable question from the boy who shared his mother's sweet tooth. Nor to a mother who, three years earlier, having convinced her mother-in-law and her friend to share their recipes with her, had the chutzpah to open a little bakery in Manhattan that specialized in cakes and pastry and that was an immediate hit even in the midst of the Depression. It was so popular that within a year there were new stores even in Flatbush and on the Grand Concourse—which she named with her own family name—Smith just being the handle she chose when she came to New York to make it as a dancer.

"And those big cookies, too?"

"Yes, Julie," Doris said, caressing the face of her blond-haired, brown-eyed four-year-old Bronx boy named for Jake's father—"black and whites too."

The Babe reached into his own Ebinger's box—courtesy of Morrie's wife—and pulled out another piece of mandel bread. Nibbling on it, slowly and carefully, he pencilled his own name in on the line-up card in the third spot, working his way down to the last line on the card—Ginsberg, pitcher, batting ninth. Shit, he chuckled to himself. Becoming manager has done wonders for my memory!

"It's time Jidge."

"Thanks kid, Get everybody together. I'll be out in a minute."

Which Philly did, as part of his responsibilities as pitching and first base coach, having given up the glove midway through the season when his knees refused to cooperate any more.

"All right boys," the Babe began, " this is what we have been playing for all season. Now I'm not one for fancy words, as you know, so let me keep it simple. Detroit, here, is a solid club from top to bottom. And that first baseman kid, what's his name. . . ."

"Greenberg, Jidge, as in Ginsberg," Morrie laughed.

"Yeah, this Greenberg kid is a terror with men on. So as long as we keep men off the bases in front of him, he's not going to hurt us. And with Master Melvin and Morrie here leading us, all we got to do is stay focused and everything will be Okee, Dokee. O. K., let's get them."

With a wave of his arm, the Babe signalled his troops to take the field, stopping Morrie as he headed for the door.

"How you feeling kid? Rested enough?"

"I'm fine Jidge, ready to go. I haven't pitched in a week."

"Don't remind me kid. Thank God that Fitzsimmons came through on Yom Kippur or you and I would both be in deep shit."

Morrie laughed. "It could have been worse. If it was today, Greenberg and I would both be in shul and the Polo Grounds would be half empty!"

"What do you mean?"

"Didn't you see the headlines today? '"Hankus Pankus versus the Rabbi of Swat!"'"

"Don't worry kid, even if you both prayed all day, this Sultan would still pack them in. Hey, I didn't mean anything about Greenberg before. I just forgot his name like I do with everyone else."

"Don't even think about it."

"Have a good one."

"Thanks Babe."

———————

———

"Good afternoon baseball fans everywhere. It's Hugh McNamee here for the National Broadcasting Company and we have a beautiful day for baseball. It's the first game of the 1934 World Series and what a match-up it should be. The National League's New York Giants versus the American League champions, the Detroit Tigers. New York's Morrie Ginsberg, The Rabbi of Swat looks in for the sign and we are under way. If you know what I mean."

John McGraw sat up in his chaise lounge and reached over to adjust the dial on his RCA Victor console so that McNamee's voice came in loud and clear. The Giant manager, resplendent in purple Bermuda shorts—a pair that he had actually picked up on the island only a few weeks before—and a short-sleeve silk shirt—sank back into the cushions, wiggled his barefoot toes in the air, and breathed deeply and freely as he tuned into baseball the way he had become accustomed to it. From his screened porch he could see the sea gulls dip and glide into the water in search of their afternoon meal. Mary would be back soon from the market and, as usual, they would have an early supper—probably grilled Pompano or scallops—before taking their usual leisurely walk to say hello to the Ringlings. The former Giant manager smiled as he contemplated his life. "Not bad Mr. McGraw, considering that a few years ago you were in debt up to your neck, your neck was on the line, and retirement to Florida seemed a distant dream. I hope Mary remembered to send that good luck telegram to the Babe. He ain't no Matty but he sure knows his baseball."

———————————

———

[I've got to hand it to you. Never mind that somehow the Giants are playing in the World Series and not St. Louis, who won it all in 1934. (Or is it 1933 and the Tigers have taken the place of the Senators?) Whatever. You've accomplished something for me that I was never able to do on my own—manage a major league ball club. Not that I didn't try to land the job. For that I thank you, even if it stretches baseball fact a bit long into fiction.

I know you are getting down to the end of this tale so I don't expect you are going to spend much time explaining how I got the job or how I did in the Series. But even the few lines you do offer suggest something of the qualities I would have brought to it if Ruppert had given me half a chance. Shit, he never looked beyond my bigness, my flamboyance—the very things that lined his pockets—to understand how much I knew about the game and how good I was with other players—something, I might add, that you do seem to understand, even if it is true that I did have trouble remembering peoples' names.

I hope you are as satisfied with how your story came out as I am with the way you've told mine, or, should I say, the way we've told mine. Thanks for the opportunity to let me put my own two cents in on my own behalf.

It's not easy to try to be honest about a person's life, whether it's someone else's or especially your own. To grapple with the complexity of circumstance and personality that shape a person's behavior, feelings, and relationships—to make a stab at comprehending somebody's life is a tall order. And just making the effort deserves some recognition. What did what's-his-name say about it? Let's see, oh yeah, 'a life unexamined is not worth living.' So hear that sound, Levine. I've crushed my last Panama hat in honor of your Rabbi of Swat.]